make money
on
eBay UK

Dan Wilson

make money
on
eBay UK

The Inside Guide to
Getting Started, Buying and Selling
Successfully on eBay.co.uk

Dan Wilson

NICHOLAS BREALEY
PUBLISHING

LONDON

First published by
Nicholas Brealey Publishing in 2005
Reprinted (twice) 2005

3–5 Spafield Street   100 City Hall Plaza, Suite 501
Clerkenwell, London   Boston
EC1R 4QB, UK   MA 02108, USA
Tel: +44 (0)20 7239 0360   Tel: (888) BREALEY
Fax: +44 (0)20 7239 0370   Fax: (617) 523 3708
                    http://www.nbrealey-books.com

ISBN 1-85788-352-7

British Library Cataloguing in Publication Data
A catalogue record for this book is available from the
British Library.

Printed in the UK by Clays Ltd, St Ives plc

Contents

1 / Welcome

Why I Love eBay

I've been trading on eBay since 1999; in fact ever since there was an eBay.co.uk to use, I've been on it. I've worked for eBay as an employee since 1999, am currently the Community Development Manager, and trade on it in my spare time too. I have more than 500 unique Feedbacks, and a 100% positive rating. If I was a contestant on *Mastermind* my chosen specialist subject would be eBay.co.uk. I know eBay inside out.

When I started working for eBay in 1999 hardly anyone in Britain had heard of it. To be honest, even I hadn't heard of it before I applied for the job and boned up for the interview. Some of my friends told me I was mad working for an internet start-up that was bound to go bust. I think some people I knew thought I was working for a porno site. And sometimes, in those early days, working for eBay was a chaotic experience: it was a young company breaking new ground, based in an office above a furniture shop in London. There was some uncertainty that we Brits could be converted to this American phenomenon.

Nowadays eBay is an established household name and it's hard not to open the papers or switch on the television or radio without seeing or hearing about eBay. Everyone has heard of it and my friends are continually asking me for trading tips and advice. But in all the time I've worked for eBay the two things that have always attracted me to it have remained constant. I am still amazed by the diversity of the people who use eBay and the astonishing variety of items for sale.

Just as I was writing this section of the book, I went off for a little ramble on eBay to see what I could find to demonstrate the huge range of items for sale. I found a stuffed squirrel wearing a little jacket, arranged in a gardening scene and sweeping away autumnal leaves. There was a life-size replica of Jean-Luc Picard from that episode of *Star Trek* when he gets turned into a Borg. I could have bid on a signed picture of Margaret Thatcher, or Michael Buerk or Ken Dodd or just about anyone you can imagine. I saw an antique dentist's chair, a signed first edition of Bill Clinton's autobiography, a box of 16 assorted glass eyes and a pair of conjoined jelly babies looking for a caring home. Where else can you find such a wonderful and amusing variety of things? Of course, eBay isn't just about the weird and wonderful – most of the stuff for sale is everyday gear available for great prices – but it's the crazy items that I find most endearing.

The other attraction for me is the diversity of the people who use eBay. It's not restricted to any particular group of people or section of society. Cherie Blair is a well-known eBay buyer, and celebrities like Sophie Ellis-Bextor, Jemima Khan and Paul Daniels are said to trade on the site. But the majority of people are just like you and me: eBay members are ordinary people from all over the country doing all sorts of jobs. The one thing they have in common is a shared interest in eBay and most of them have a fun story to tell about their trading. If you want to start a conversation with an eBay member, all you need to ask is 'What's your Feedback score?' and soon you'll be jabbering away nineteen to the dozen. Fellow members will often tell you about a fabulous bargain or a particularly lucrative sale. Members like to boast about glowing Feedback they have received or amazing sellers who have provided brilliant service.

Of the people I meet, the ones I like best are those who have changed their lives by selling on eBay and making money in a way they never imagined possible. I've met single mums who make ends meet through eBay selling and retired people who help their pensions go further by clearing out their clutter. Others have chucked in the day job and make a living by selling on the site. And for most of them it's been a step up: they are making more money than ever and they have the pleasure of working for themselves. The passion and enthusiasm that these sellers have for eBay is always inspiring and makes me feel that the work I do is worthwhile.

So that's why I love eBay: there's nothing else like it in the world. You can trade all sorts of things with all sorts of people. You can make money and buy bargains from the comfort of your own home and also get your hands on things you never imagined you would find. I hope that once you've read this book and started making money on eBay you'll be as enthusiastic about it as I am.

Why You Need This Book

Time and again I've met people who want to buy and sell on eBay, they are just a little bit scared that they'll mess up or find it all a bit tricky. 'What I need,' they say, 'is someone to take me through it, to show me how it works.'

I will introduce you to the eBay.co.uk website and guide you step by step. I will show you how to register, find an item you want to buy and how to make your first purchases, before showing you how to sell your first item. I've tried to make the guide easy to understand by avoiding internet jargon and technobabble.

This book is about mastering the basic skills and giving you the knowledge you will need to get started on eBay. It will also awaken you to a world of potential for people who want to make serious money. Have you ever considered quitting your job and setting up on your own? It's possible on eBay. I can't transform you into the next Richard Branson overnight, but you will learn how to buy and sell on eBay with confidence.

Once you have learnt how eBay works you can use it to make money. The possibilities are endless. If you have things you don't use any more, why not sell them rather than chuck them out or leave them gathering dust in the shed? Or you can buy things at car boot sales, jumble sales, even on the High Street and sell them on eBay at a profit. All you need is a computer with internet access.

Here's an example of how I made money on eBay. In the January sales I spotted three life-size cardboard cut-outs of Buffy the Vampire Slayer in a well-known High Street shop. They'd originally been priced at £14.99 but they'd been reduced to £3. I snapped them up and put them on eBay that evening. After a week I'd sold them for nearly £20 each. You are probably passing up opportunities just like this every day.

Some people are put off eBay because they have read in the newspapers that it's an unsafe place to trade where people get ripped off. Bad news is good news – ask any newspaper editor. Every now and again you read an article about someone who has fallen for a scam or sent money to a seller but didn't receive the item they had paid for. I'm not going to pretend that there aren't some bad apples on eBay who want to rip people off. Unfortunately there are a small number of people who are dishonest. This is true of any marketplace, whether it's a car boot sale, an antiques fair or a local street market: there are a few dodgy dealers who want to get their hands on your money by any means possible.

Remember this: you don't need to be a victim. You can protect yourself by using your common sense and the protection programmes and safety features that eBay has in place. I've bought hundreds of things on eBay. In fact I check eBay first whenever I need something. I've bought furniture, vintage vinyl, cornish pasties, razor blades, CDs, DVDs, videos, antique prints, shoes, hats and computer equipment and I've never been ripped off. Not once.

This is because I know what to look out for and what to avoid. You'll find a chapter about trading safely later in the book. I've also included safety advice and tips wherever I can. I bet you don't know that if you buy an item on eBay that's protected by the PayPal Buyer Protection Programme, you can claim back up to £500 if you don't get the item. All this, and more, is outlined right here in this book.

Whenever you see something billed as Inside Information, you'll find my thoughts and opinions on a particular aspect of eBay. They are totally personal and you might disagree with me. You'll also find tips and interesting facts dotted through the book.

The internet and eBay are always changing. This book is current and the principles of selling on eBay will never change, but by the time you read it some of the details might be different. It's always worth checking on the eBay site for the most up-to-date information.

Inside Information:
What Is the eBay Community?

I am the Community Development Manager at eBay. But what do I mean by community? You're going to see the word a lot in this book, so it's worth being clear on what it means from the start.

Community as a word isn't used in Britain with quite the same ease and enthusiasm as it is in America. If you think about it, in the UK it is often used in not-so-positive ways. Think of the community charge, care in the community or community service.

But on eBay it's an overwhelmingly positive word and concept. In fact, it is eBay. You can't have eBay without the eBay community. It just wouldn't work.

On eBay the community is all the buyers and sellers on the site as well as the staff that eBay employs to maintain the marketplace. But it's not just about the fact that we're all on eBay happily doing our own things in isolation. The power of community is that we're all looking out for each other. Being part of any community is about realising that your actions can have a positive effect on other people.

The other strength of being part of a community is that members are in charge of what is bought and sold. eBay as an organisation doesn't direct the trading on the site. Prices are set by buyers and sellers. It's those in the community who do all the buying and selling. eBay doesn't hold any stock itself. eBay doesn't say 'a sprocket is worth £4', it's only worth £4 if is someone is willing to bid that much.

So for employees, thinking in terms of a community is vital if eBay is to survive and prosper. The CEO of eBay encourages staff to keep the community 'front and centre' in our minds. As employees we must be respectful of the needs of buyers as well as sellers while we go about our jobs and make sure we look after everyone on eBay so that the vibrant trading environment is preserved.

This is why eBay takes the views of the community seriously and consults members and traders more fully than most other companies. You can see the community interacting every day on the Discussion Boards and staff like to keep an eye on these so they can get a feel for what those in the community are saying.

And you should take it seriously too as you get started on eBay. Your eBay trading experience and success are dependent on other members of the community. If you check someone's Feedback you are checking the views of other members; one day you might go to the Discussion Boards for advice, which will be freely given by other members; you'll be buying from other members of the community too and selling to them. All that binds it together is the power of the community.

We're in this eBay thing together: you, me and more than a hundred million other people too. We are the eBay community and that's kinda cool.

How eBay Began

When you look at eBay today you will find more than one hundred million members worldwide, millions of items for sale and thousands of people making a living from selling on it. It is astonishing to think it was only started in 1995. Nowadays eBay is a household name, but it all began as a labour of love in a spare bedroom.

Pierre Omidyar looked like a stereotypical geek with his ponytail, glasses and goatee beard. He was an early convert to the new technology of the internet and worked as a computer programmer in Silicon Valley, California. In his spare time he created his own computer programs and chatted with other net heads in newsgroups and chatrooms. But he was by no means a loser. He was keen to explore the possibilities the internet would offer as it became more widely used.

In the mid-1990s the internet boom was just beginning and pioneering businesspeople were desperately trying to make millions from the new technology. Pierre stands out as a very different figure.

The legend goes that one evening over dinner at home Pierre's fiancée Pam mentioned that it was difficult to find people to trade Pez dispensers with. The couple had recently moved from Boston to California, where Pam lacked a circle of fellow collectors with whom to trade the plastic sweet dispensers.

Spurred on and keen to solve the problem, Pierre set up eBay so that Pam could interact and trade with other Pez enthusiasts online. That is the touching legend of how eBay was born, although it isn't the whole truth.

Like so many others in California, Pierre was excited by the new potential of the internet. And like the other entrepreneurs in Silicon Valley, he was looking for the 'big idea'. Pierre was different because he was interested in the way the internet could transform how people traded with each other. He wanted to apply his programming skills to an old problem in a whole new way: he wanted to create the perfect marketplace.

How Pierre Broke the Mould

Even though the Pez story of eBay's creation isn't the complete story, it does colourfully illustrate the revolutionary way in which eBay broke the mould. Other pioneering ecommerce businesses were striving to establish traditional businesses online. Amazon was applying the usual bookselling formula and offering bargains because it didn't have the expense of shops, for instance.

But eBay isn't a retailer. Pierre wasn't simply trying to create an online shop and sell lots of things to a willing online public. He was creating a marketplace where other people would come together to trade with each other. eBay wasn't set up so Pez could sell directly to Pam; rather, the aim was to provide a venue for people like Pam to buy and sell with each other.

The idea of creating a marketplace is hardly a new one. Trading is an innately human activity. However, the fact that the idea could be revolutionised by the internet intrigued Pierre. The biggest attraction for him was that the normal rules no longer applied. An online marketplace could have a potentially huge impact not least because geography no longer mattered. On the internet information can cross the planet in the twinkling of an eye.

The Perfect Market

Pierre's expectation was that over time the number of people who would have access to the internet would be huge. Internet aficionados were a fairly small bunch in 1995, but as the number of households with personal computers grew the web's use was bound to expand.

More exciting was the fact that the rules of the 'real world' didn't have to apply. Pierre could start from scratch and create an unfettered marketplace. Existing marketplaces (stock exchanges or the oil market, for instance) benefited bigger players and established traders. Prices and conditions were fixed to favour vested interests. It was rarely possible for outsiders to compete fairly.

Pierre's belief was that a marketplace had to be as free as possible to be truly effective. He also believed that prices were better set by buyers rather than sellers. After all, what is a fair market price other than what someone is readily willing to pay? This belief was central to Pierre's affection for auctions.

In an auction sellers are able to set the minimum price they are willing to accept and if someone thinks that is a fair price they will buy. If two or more people are willing to pay the price, or more, they bid against each other until the highest price they are willing to pay is established. The fair market price is set by buyers on the basis of what they think something is worth rather than by outside controls, cartels or vested interests.

AuctionWeb's Early Days

Over the course of the Labor Day weekend in 1995, Pierre wrote an auction program and added it to his existing website. It was a simple affair allowing people to add items for sale, view the items and bid on them. Pierre's website, which was already called eBay, also hosted pages for his fiancée and an offbeat tribute to the deadly Ebola virus. Pierre added what he called 'AuctionWeb' to the site that weekend and set about publicising it to other internet users in newsgroups and chatrooms.

Why eBay Is Called eBay

So Pierre called his first auction experiment AuctionWeb and it could be reached via the address www.ebay.com/aw. In due course AuctionWeb simply became known as eBay – but where did the word eBay come from?

There are all sorts of theories. The most famous myth suggests that because eBay was started in the Bay Area of California, eBay stands for East Bay. But it was actually started in Campbell, near San Jose, which is really the South Bay area, so that theory doesn't hold much water.

Another theory harks back to an age when clippers circumnavigated the globe carrying exotic cargoes from faraway places. In those days a bay was a place of safety and security where trade was possible. The e in eBay denotes the fact that this safe harbour for trade is online.

The truth seems to owe rather more to luck than judgement. Pierre wanted to call his website EchoBay.com simply because he thought it sounded cool. When he went to register the site he discovered that the name had already been taken by a Canadian mining company. eBay.com was apparently still available so, deciding it was the next best thing, he snapped it up. In an age where multinational corporations spend hundreds of thousands of pounds on focus groups and research to decide which shade of blue they should use in their logo, it is amusing to think that one of the most popular brand names in the world was created on a whim.

> *Fact*: Pierre claims that he realised eBay was going to be huge when he sold a broken laser pointer for $14.

eBay Takes Off

In the latter months of 1995 Pierre spent his time developing the auction website by adding new functions and features and advertising it to other web users. He was astonished by the number of people who started flocking to the site to buy and sell. The most powerful marketing tool was the group of happy users who told their friends about the great new website that let you buy and sell to anyone else online.

In the very early days eBay was free. For Pierre it was just a hobby and he was content to let people trade for no fee, but inevitably his costs started to rise. His internet service provider was concerned by the amount of traffic his site was getting and started to charge him commercial rates for hosting his website. Reluctantly Pierre realised that he had to receive payment for the service, so he created a system that meant that sellers who successfully sold items paid him a very small percentage of the price they got to help him cover his costs.

He was amazed when people readily paid him what they owed. Typically they were small amounts, but they all added up to cover his running costs. Soon he was receiving so many payments that he was making a little profit and he could barely keep up with the flood of receipts: many were left unprocessed for days because he was too busy to open the envelopes.

People Are Basically Good

As eBay grew Pierre firmly imprinted it with his own beliefs and philosophy. Inevitably there were sometimes disputes between trading partners, who looked to him to resolve their disagreements. It became apparent that most of the problems were simple cases of misunderstanding. People were reading the worst into the emails they received, convinced that other members were trying to rip them off or do them over.

Pierre encouraged aggrieved traders to resolve problems between themselves, firmly believing that people are basically good. They shouldn't jump to the wrong conclusion and immediately think the worst, but rather try to see the issue from another point of view and seek a mutually beneficial arrangement. His belief was reinforced as he watched complete strangers buying and selling with each other every day. People sent money in the post to others they had never met and received their purchases in return. In comparison to the successful transactions, the number of disputes was extremely small.

The Power of Community

Pierre was so confident in his belief that people are basically good that he came up with a way of making it a feature of the eBay site. He wanted to make the good trades count and show that they far outweighed the bad ones. He created a system that became eBay's greatest selling point and most distinguishing feature: Feedback. He invited people on eBay to make comments about their fellow traders. These comments were then crystallised as a record of a member's reputation and conduct on the site. Good trading experiences could be marked with positive Feedback. If sellers had conducted themselves well and delivered the item well packaged and swiftly, positive Feedback comments were appropriate. For buyers a swift payment would qualify them for a positive.

If a transaction was not satisfactory then negative Feedback could be left. For instance, if a seller received payment but didn't send the goods or if a buyer didn't pay for purchases, then negative Feedback might be the best course of action. From the beginning Pierre encouraged people to settle their differences before leaving a negative. Feedback was a permanent record of a person's dealing on eBay so a negative left in haste would remain for others to see.

For Pierre the main strength of Feedback was its openness. It allowed traders to make public what they thought. They had to be honest and relate it to their own experience. Moreover, people were discouraged from leaving personal remarks. By keeping Feedback factual and relevant it became a useful source of information for other members.

Feedback was about empowering eBay's members so they could help each other. If a member had stacks of positive Feedback, other members were encouraged to trade with them. If a member had some positive and some negative Feedback, it might pay others to be cautious. People with a lot of negative Feedback were simply avoided. But Feedback thrived because people are basically good. It feels good to give a compliment and leave positive Feedback and to this day that forms the central tenet of trust on eBay.

Further evidence that people are basically good came from the generosity members showed each other on eBay's Discussion Boards. Early on Pierre provided a forum for members to interact that served several useful functions. It meant he could distance himself from the site. Rather than being seen as dictatorial and controlling, he preferred to be hands-off and allow the community of users to chart the course of the business.

More importantly, people could help each other solve any difficulties they faced as they traded. A core of dedicated and experienced members frequented the boards and when someone was new or unsure they could ask for help and receive it from another member. Fellow members were generous when it came to offering advice on trading, help with HTML for item listings or information on how to display a picture that showed the item being sold.

One early community member using the boards was Jim Griffith, who advised fellow eBayers under his self-created alter-ego: Uncle Griff. The invented character of Griff was a cross-dressing farmer dominated by his mother and he dished out help and advice in a humorous and self-deprecating way that immediately defused antagonism and put people at ease.

Griffith became the first of eBay's customer support reps in 1996. eBay had started to receive a large number of emails every day from members who wanted help and someone was needed to answer them. Griffith was the obvious choice and he continued to post on the Discussion Boards and answer emails as well as buying and selling on eBay.

eBay's community ethos is something that sets it apart from most other companies. It remains central to the identity of eBay and how it operates. The community is consulted on decisions and members' comments are fed back to executives on a daily basis. In return, the eBay community is not shy in giving its opinions. When a change to the site is implemented, employees can often be found poring over the Discussion Boards looking for compliments or complaints.

The eBay Phenomenon

By 1996 eBay was already very successful. Not only was the site attracting buyers and sellers at an astonishing rate, but Pierre had to hire people to help him to maintain the site and its momentum. In these early years eBay was predominantly a site for collectors and collectables and its reputation as a great venue for buying and selling was mainly spread by word of mouth.

It became clear that if eBay was to realise its true potential it would have to become a more professional and conventional organisation. Pierre had always run the business in an egalitarian way and was attracted to hiring people with a similar counterculture mindset, but he came to realise that a more sober selection of experienced professionals was required to complement them. To begin with some graduates of the Stanford Business School were engaged to offer marketing expertise, and soon eBay was advertising its service on AOL using banner ads.

The next logical step was to hire a professional Chief Executive Officer to take over the running of the business from Pierre. He was perhaps rare as a founder of a successful company in realising that his skills and ambitions were not best suited to running what was fast becoming a big and complicated organisation. eBay found its CEO in the unusual figure of Meg Whitman, who could not have been more unlike Pierre. She was a Princeton and Harvard graduate from old East Coast stock. She had experience working for some of the biggest companies in America: Procter and Gamble, Bain, Disney, Stride Rite and Hasbro. Even though she didn't have much online experience and was by no means a techie, she saw eBay's potential and brought with her vast marketing experience that would be critical to the company's success. Most important of all, she understood the importance of the community when it came to driving eBay's success.

Soon after Meg came to eBay, the decision was made to go public and offer shares on the Nasdaq stock exchange. At the peak of the internet boom going public was the ultimate badge of credibility for internet start-ups. It sent a message that a company was serious and meant to stay the distance. Equally, issuing shares to the public was a useful way of raising money to continue investing in the company, although in eBay's case this was less important. Looking back there were lots of companies for whom going public was the peak of their success: many went bust within months of floating.

For eBay going public was a tricky proposition. Obviously the business was already profitable and successful and had a million members and millions of items being traded. But it was difficult explaining to stuffy bankers that people are basically good and really are willing to trade with complete strangers on the internet. Was eBay just a fad? Did it truly have a broad appeal that would enable it to grow? eBay was valued at about $715 million on the day before its shares went on the market in September 1998. By the end of the first day's trading it was obvious that the market liked eBay and thought it would be a huge success. So much so, in fact, that trading was brisk and at the end of the first day eBay's valuation stood at $2 billion.

eBay Goes Global

In 1999 eBay began to take the site to a wider international audience. Millions of people were already trading on eBay in 1999 and not all of them were American. People from all over the world were using eBay.com to trade wherever they lived. But to succeed, it would be necessary to create sites in local languages moulded to the needs of the community members in that country.

The first move was to buy Alando.de, a German online trading site that closely resembled eBay in its community-based approach. Alando had been started by a group of young entrepreneurs barely months before. It caught eBay's eye and Pierre travelled to Berlin to have a closer look. He was impressed by Alando and struck by the similarities between it and eBay, so he bought the company. The site was rebranded as eBay.de and by the end of the year eBay members could trade in German marks. eBay sites were also established in Australia and Canada.

In Britain there was no site similar to eBay that could be purchased, so eBay started from scratch and created eBay.co.uk. There was already a core of UK members who traded on eBay.com in US dollars. Sellers would sell uniquely British collectables and goods to Americans, who in return would pay in cash. In those early days there were thousands of envelopes stuffed with cash crossing the Atlantic paying for items that were hard to find in America. In July 1999 people in Britain became able for the first time to trade on eBay in sterling rather than dollars. A UK office was set up to start building the eBay.co.uk site for British traders and to market it by attracting buyers and sellers. In those early days QXL was stiff competition in the UK market, but the draw of eBay became too much for the ever-growing number of Brits who wanted to buy and sell online, and before long eBay became the number one ecommerce site in Britain.

Success You Can Share

This book is about how to make money on eBay. It might sound like the story of how eBay began is the story of how a small group of Americans became very rich, but what jumps out are the millions of people who have made eBay what it is today. All the selling on eBay is done by members; all eBay runs is the marketplace. It brings in buyers and makes sure everything is running smoothly, but eBay is only successful if its sellers and their sales are successful. eBay doesn't make a bean unless people sell on the site, so eBay's profits are a reflection of the wider success of eBay sellers.

> *Fact*: The most expensive item ever bought on eBay was a Gulfstream jet, which sold for $4.9 million. One of Mrs Thatcher's handbags sold for more than £100,000.

In 2003, 971 million items valued at a total of $24 billion were sold by eBay's sellers in 150 countries. eBay continues to expand into new markets and develop the websites to reflect the needs of traders and help them be more successful. There is a market out there for you to tap. You can share in eBay's success by taking advantage of a unique audience that you cannot reach in any other way.

Now is a great time to get involved with the eBay phenomenon. Never before have there been so many buyers on eBay. eBay has never before been investing so much in advertising and development. You too can join in eBay's success, become a seller and make money from the world's biggest marketplace.

2

Getting Started

If you have a computer and internet access, you'll be able to use eBay. A basic computer and a 56k dial-up connection will do just fine. But as with any website, a faster connection and a better set-up will make your experience more enjoyable. Obviously, if you plan to use eBay to make serious money, a broadband connection could be a very sound investment, saving you time and money in the long run.

- **Email address** You can use any email address you want to register with eBay, but try to choose one with plenty of storage that you can access wherever you are. Some people set up a specific email address for their eBay use to keep it separate from their other mail.

- **Internet browser** eBay is optimised to be compatible with the most up-to-date version of Internet Explorer. If you are using an old version of the browser (or a different browser altogether) you might find it difficult to use eBay. To ensure you have the current version of Internet Explorer you should visit www.microsoft.com.

- **Mac users** eBay is accessible using an Apple Macintosh. But do note that some of the advanced facilities such as Turbo Lister are not available for Macs.

- **Web TV** You can access eBay using Web TV, but it is not ideal and the site will not work as it would on a PC. Buying is possible but selling will be very difficult and adding pictures to your listings impossible. Your best bet would be to get hold of an affordable PC or try accessing eBay via an internet café or your local library.

• **Peripherals** A printer is not essential but it will make your life a lot easier. When you become a seller you may well want to invest in a scanner or a digital camera, but as a buyer you will have no need for these when using eBay.

• **AOL users** If you use AOL you need to type 'eBay' into the Keyword box on your AOL homepage.

The eBay Homepage

eBay's web address or URL is www.ebay.co.uk. As with any website, you simply type the address into the browser window, press 'go' and you will be taken to the site.

The first page you'll see on eBay is the visitor homepage. This is a special homepage for people who have never visited before and gives you an introduction to eBay. You only see this the first time you visit. After that you will see eBay's regular homepage.

The homepage has links to everywhere you need to visit on eBay. On the lefthand side you can see the categories where people list their items for sale. If you want to browse the items for sale you can click on the heading you want. The top section is the Navigation Bar, which takes you to other sections of the site. From here you can access My eBay (where eBay provides a list of all your buying and selling activities), the Site Map and the Sell Your Item form. There's also a link to eBay's Help section. On the Navigation Bar at the top of the page you will also see the Register button. If you click on this you will be taken to the Registration Form.

Tip: Make eBay your Homepage

You can make eBay your personal homepage. This means that every time you log on to the internet the first page you see will be eBay. To make eBay your homepage simply click the 'Start' button at the bottom left of your screen. In the Menu, select 'Settings' and click on the 'Control Panel' option. In the Control

Panel you should choose 'Internet Options' and a grey box will pop up.

In the space for an address enter 'www.ebay.co.uk' and click 'OK' at the base of the box. Now you'll be taken to eBay every time you log on to the internet.

Registering with eBay

You can surf around the eBay site and look at the items for sale without registering, but you will not be able to buy or sell. Becoming a member is straightforward and won't take long.

To register with eBay you will need to click the 'Register' button in the Navigation Bar on the homepage. This will take you to the Registration Form.

The first step of registering with eBay is to provide your personal and contact details. Obviously these are kept confidential and secure. eBay doesn't sell your personal information to other companies or third parties. You can find out more about how eBay will store your information by reading the Privacy Policy. You will need to fill in your name, address and telephone number. You can also add a second telephone number or fax number, but this is not compulsory.

It is very important that you put in correct personal details and valid contact information. If these details are false you will be suspended from eBay without warning and have to go through the rigmarole of confirming your identity to eBay by providing domestic bills and ID like a passport or driving licence, which can be time consuming and irritating.

- **Email address** eBay communicates with its members via email, so it is important that you provide an email address to which you have regular access. You will need to type it in twice to confirm it is correct.

- **Choosing a User ID** Once you have entered your personal details you will need to select a User ID. This is the name that you will operate under on eBay and is rather like a CB 'handle' or alias. It's a really good opportunity to show off and choose a name that reflects your personality or interests. Take a look around the site at other users

eb Y.co.uk

Registration: Enter Information Help

1 **Enter Information**   2 Agree to Terms   3 Check Your Email

First name

Last name

Street address

Town / City

County
— England —

Postal code

Country
United Kingdom
Change country

Primary telephone
( )

Secondary telephone (Optional)
( )

Important: To complete registration, enter a valid email address that you can check immediately.

Email address

Examples: myname@yahoo.com, myname@example.com, etc.

Re-enter email address

Create your eBay User ID

Example: rose789 (Don't use your email address)
Your User ID identifies you to other eBay users.

Create password

6-character minimum
Enter a password that's easy for you to remember, but hard for others to guess. See tips.

Re-enter password

Secret question
Pick a suggested question...

Secret answer

You will be asked for the answer to your secret question if you forget your password.

Date of birth
—Day—   —Month—   Year

Continue >

and see what kind of User IDs they use. With so many members on eBay already there is a strong chance that your first choice of User ID has already been taken, so you will need to be inventive. If the first User ID you choose is not available, eBay will guide you through choosing a different ID.

• **Password** You will also need to choose your password. You should select a password that will be easy for you to remember and impossible for other people to guess. Avoid using 'password' or your User ID as your password. Don't use anything obviously relating to you either, such as your name or your partner's name. Try to use a mix of letters and numbers and also include lower- and upper-case letters. You can make this easier to remember by using numbers as if they are letters: 'z00k33pEr' or 'Dilligent'. You can find out more about keeping your password safe later in the book.

• **Secret question** At the bottom of the registration page you will also need to set your secret question. This is a question that only you will know the answer to. In the event that you forget your password, eBay will require your secret answer to reset it. The questions include 'What street did you grow up on?' and 'What is the name of your first school?'

• **Confirming your registration** When you have completed all the sections on the Registration Form you will be taken to the next page, where you will be asked to accept and agree to eBay's User Agreement and Privacy Policy. You can print these out so you can peruse them more easily. Once you have agreed to the terms, you will be sent an email. This email is eBay's way of checking that the email address you have provided is correct. When you receive the email you should click the 'Confirm Registration' button inside. You will be taken to eBay and will then be a fully registered eBay member ready to use the site.

• **Anonymous email addresses** eBay takes safety very seriously and one way it protects the people who are buying and selling on the site is to require a credit or debit card from people who are registering with anonymous email accounts.

If you want to register using an anonymous email account such as Hotmail or Yahoo, you will need to provide credit or debit card information. Don't worry: your personal details will be kept confidential and your card will never be charged without your consent. eBay just wants to know that you are who you say you are.

• **What if my email doesn't arrive?** If you register on eBay and you don't get the confirmation email immediately, sit tight. The email can take up to 24 hours to arrive. If after a day you haven't received it, it is wise to request that eBay sends it again. You can request this via the link on the Site Map.

If you have to request your email again the chances are that your email provider is to blame. You may have your email account security settings set so high that you can only receive emails from senders pre-approved by you. If your security settings are in order and you still haven't received the email, you should contact your email provider or internet service provider for advice.

Tip: User IDs

Your User ID is a key part of your eBay personality. Take a moment to think about what you want your User ID to be and what you want it to say. Don't forget that as a buyer, and more importantly as a seller, it says something about you and can influence people. A good User ID will attract other eBay members, but one with dodgy overtones might well put people off trading with you.

Some people like to choose a User ID that reflects a part of their character or represents something they aspire to or admire. Some select a favourite character from a soap opera or film. Others will opt for a pun, but some are very professional and opt for a name that is relevant to their buying or selling interest. Just take a look around eBay and you will see all sorts of IDs for all sorts of people.

If you have an idea for an ID and want to see if it is already taken by someone else, you can use the eBay Search facility to check it out. Click 'Advanced Search' on the righthand side of the Navigation Bar on the homepage and go for the 'Search by Seller' tab. Type in the ID you would like and if it isn't taken eBay will tell you that the 'User ID isn't recognised'.

PART 1

BUYING ON eBAY

3

What Can I Buy on eBay?

The answer is just about anything. To start with there are new and nearly new goods. eBay is great for CDs, DVDs and videos. You can often pick them up for far less than you would in the shops. Clothing is also a very popular purchase. Many sellers take pride in offering clothes at a fraction of what High Street vendors charge. Try eBay both for cutting-edge items that are hard to find in the shops and vintage or retro clothing. You can also get hold of designer labels at a good price.

eBay also has hundreds of thousands of different household items such as DVD players, CD players, fun items like iPods, computer-related gear (both hardware and software) and just about any sort of appliance you can imagine. Many of these items are brand new or nearly new. Lots of people sell unwanted gifts or things they don't really need. Every year after Christmas eBay is the first stop for lots of people who want to sell that pointless gift from Auntie Maud, so that's a great time to pick up a new item at a bargain price.

Second Hand, Antique and Collectable

When eBay started in the US in the 1990s, it was immediately seized on by collectors. It was the perfect marketplace for collectables: collectors in Maine could get together with others in California and buy and sell. In the early days Beanie Baby enthusiasts dominated eBay and it quickly became the place that people crazy to get their hands on a new bear would visit.

Collectables are still hugely popular on eBay. Just have a browse through the Collectables section to see the breadth of items for sale. You can buy old theatre posters, cigarette cards, football programmes, porcelain, enamel advertising signs and glass bottles. If you are building a collection, the chances are that eBay will have something you are looking for.

It is also an excellent place to get your hands on antiques of all kinds. Whether you fancy a Victorian oil painting or engraving, a Regency table or some exquisite silverware, it can all be found on eBay. Many reputable antiques traders operate on eBay and are happy to organise postage and insurance at very competitive rates.

Oddities and curios are an eBay speciality. If you want to get an antique eyebath, a taxidermy mongoose, a bottle of water from the Princess Diana Memorial Fountain or a smutty postcard, eBay has them all by the dozen.

Local, National, International

The icing on the eBay cake is the option buyers have to trade with sellers all over the world. Not only can you buy from sellers in the UK, but from just about every country in the world. This means that you can source goods from faraway places that might otherwise be out of reach.

And if you want to stay local, you can. You can choose to buy from British members only and you can select sellers from your immediate area. Buying locally is convenient and straight-forward. This is ideal if you want a bulky item that would be expensive to post or something perishable that needs to be sent quickly.

Not just Auctions

eBay is most famous for its traditional auction format where buyers place bids against each other and the highest bidder wins. But eBay isn't just about auctions. You can use the 'Buy It Now' option too. This is where you buy an item at a price specified by the seller. You don't bid against other bidders and you don't have to wait until the auction ends. If you want to make an immediate purchase you can use this feature.

Inside Information:
But I Want to Make Money, Not Spend It!

Hold your horses. The simple fact is that people who jump straight into selling don't tend to make a success of it. You need to learn about the eBay marketplace and the features it can offer you before taking the plunge. Without doubt the best way to learn about eBay is to experience it as a buyer.

Your First Purchase

Once you have registered on eBay, you are ready to start buying. But what is available? The answer is pretty much everything. eBay has sellers all over the world selling all kinds of things. You'll be surprised by what you can find.

When making your first purchase, it's really advisable to make it safe and easy so you can learn the process. Don't rush in and bid on an exotic item from Ghana. Choose a cheaper item located in the UK to gain confidence. Once you are happy with how eBay works for buyers, the sky's the limit. You can get on with buying cars, antiques, holidays and other big-ticket items when you are an experienced buyer.

Inside Information:
People Really Are Basically Good

If the doom-mongers had their way there would be no such thing as eBay. It shouldn't work. It's based on a belief that people are basically good and they will be as good as their word. Who, apart from some idealistic tie-dyed ageing hippie, would believe that you could send money to a complete stranger and in return you would receive the item you have bought?

And that's what is so wonderful about eBay: it proves that people really are basically good and trustworthy. That's not to say there aren't a few bad apples out there. It is inevitable that there will be some people who set out to scam you and rip you off.

The majority of transactions that occur every day on eBay are successful for buyer and seller alike. Think about it: eBay couldn't survive unless almost every trade was successful and safe, it would be out of business. To date over 2.3 billion transactions have taken place on eBay, and if that isn't proof that people are basically good I don't know what is.

Trust is manifested in eBay's Feedback system. A member's Feedback score is all the reviews that other members have left after a trade. Buyers leave them for sellers and vice versa. These comments are totally open and available for everyone to see. Feedback is a person's eBay reputation and something eBay members take very seriously. It is the number one thing that builds and reinforces trust on eBay.

When you are finding your feet as a buyer, go with someone you trust. Take a look at a seller's Feedback. Check out their item descriptions. Look at their About Me page. You'll be amazed how many lovely people there are out there. On eBay there are many more nice people than nasty ones.

Learn how eBay Works

Treat your first purchase on eBay as a way to learn. Buying isn't difficult but it is a bit different from using other ecommerce sites. You will most likely be dealing with an individual rather than a big business. eBay also has things like Feedback and PayPal with which you might be unfamiliar. By taking your time to learn and absorb eBay's foibles, you'll be in a great position to successfully buy on the site again and again. Taking a few moments now to learn about eBay might save you hours of hassle later.

Choose a Kind Seller

Try to find a seller who will help you through your first purchase. Most sellers on eBay are individuals who will be happy to guide you if you are unsure or need a nudge in the right direction. It is worth telling a seller that you are taking the plunge on their item.

Most sellers will be delighted to assist an eBay newbie and many will go out of their way to be helpful and friendly.

Be Prepared

Don't forget to be prepared. Once a listing is over many sellers like to get moving quickly, so you'll need to be ready to pay and receive the item. Make sure you are able to pay using a method acceptable to the seller. It might also be worth opening a PayPal account prior to placing your first bid. To register with PayPal, you need to go to www.paypal.co.uk; there is more on this later in the book.

4

Finding an Item You Want to Buy

There are millions of items for sale, so finding an item you want to buy can be a little daunting. This chapter will show you how to find the item you want with speed and ease. There are two ways of finding items on eBay: Browsing and Searching.

Browsing on eBay reflects how you would use a department store. If you wanted a new lamp you would go to the Lighting section of the homeware area of the shop. The same is true on eBay. You would go to the Family, Home and Garden category and look in the Lamps section. Or if you were after something antique you would go to the Antiques section. Browsing is the way to find an item if you know what you want but are flexible about the style, brand and type.

Searching offers a way of finding items in a more focused way. If you have a brand, specs, dimensions or a particular item in mind, you can use eBay's search engine to search the items for sale in the same way you would use Google to search the internet.

Browsing

The items for sale on eBay are divided into categories. Sellers choose the categories they want their items to appear in when they put them up for sale.

If you want to browse eBay there are two ways to get started. On the homepage you will find the full list of top-level categories on the lefthand side. Simply click on the category you are interested in, such as 'Collectables' or 'PC and Video Games', and you will be taken to the Category Index page of that category. From here you can start browsing lower-level categories, leading you to the item you want to buy.

You can also browse by clicking on 'Buy' in the Navigation Bar on most pages. This link will lead you to a full list of top-level categories and the next level down. To find a Scrabble set, for example, you'd go for the category 'Toys & Games' and on the Category Index page you'll see a heading 'Games & Puzzles' with a subheading 'Board Games'.

When you click on the 'Board Games' link you will be taken to a list of all the items in the 'Board Games' category. There are almost certainly some Scrabble sets in this section, but because this is a big category you'll have to look through dozens of pages to find them. It will be much quicker to use the lefthand column and narrow down the results. There is a further list of sub-categories for you to choose from. In this case 'Scrabble' will probably be the best choice. Don't forget that not all sellers will have had the good sense to put their Scrabble set in the 'Scrabble' category, so it could be worth having a look in 'Other Board Games' too just in case.

Browsing is a great way of discovering the enormous array of items for sale on eBay. It is also ideal if you know you want to buy something but don't have a concrete idea of the exact item you're looking for.

A full list of categories on the site can be found at http://listings.ebay.co.uk/.

Searching

eBay has a very efficient search engine that will take you directly to items if you have a keyword or phrase. If you want to find a Blur-related single and it doesn't matter whether it's on CD, tape or vinyl, or if you're interested in Peter Cook and want to see all related items, then searching will be the more efficient way of finding an item. When you put a keyword or phrase into eBay's search engine, such as 'Wedgwood', all items with that word or phrase in the Item Title will be returned for you to look through.

You can use the search engine for single words or combinations of words.

If too many items are returned to you and you want to enter a more specific term (say 'Wedgwood plate' rather than just 'Wedgwood'), simply click 'Back' on your browser and start again.

Tips: Searching

There are a number of tricks you can use to make the search engine work for you and find the items you really want. If you put 'loch ness monster' in the search engine you will get every item with those words in the title: anything with the words 'loch', 'ness' and 'monster' will be returned regardless of what order they appear in the title. So you might also get a 'Loch Fyne Monster Bundle, Van Ness' alongside 'Loch Ness Monster Legends Book'.

If you are specifically interested in the Loch Ness monster and want to use the search engine to find the exact phrase, you need to enclose your search term in inverted commas like this: "loch ness monster". This will only return items with the words in the correct order; you can do this for any phrase.

If you are more interested in Loch Ness memorabilia but have absolutely no interest in the monster, you can instruct the search engine to search for Loch Ness but exclude any results that include the word monster. You do this by placing a minus sign before the word you want to exclude: loch ness –monster.

If you want to exclude a number of words you can do that too. So you might still be after those Loch Ness items but don't want anything to do with the monster and are averse to haggis and whisky too. You would use the command: loch ness –(monster,haggis,whisky).

You can also widen your search by including Item Descriptions as well as Titles. To do this simply click on the 'Search Titles and Descriptions' option underneath the Search box.

Finding Bargains

There *are* bargains out there. Some bargains are intentional, coming from sellers who revel in being able to undercut rivals and who offer quality items at a low price. Others are accidental. The accidental bargain is usually being sold by a bewildered seller who cannot understand why their treasure hasn't reached the price it really deserves. Typically the seller has made an error in the listing or failed to include something in the Title or Description that means buyers cannot track the item down.

Take note of these common errors so you know where to look for a bargain on eBay. But make sure you don't commit the same mistakes yourself when you start selling.

- **Sellers who don't know what they've got** Every now and again you'll see something on eBay that is rare and spectacular. If the seller doesn't know it is a really desirable object, the title will be vague and the description will lack details. This is where trawling the site for an 'old pot', a 'nice vase' or an 'interesting picture' can reap rewards. 99% of the results will be boring things of no particular interest or value. But one day the poorly titled item will be a treasure.

- **Bad titles and spelling mistakes** When someone lists an item with a poor title, buyers won't be able to find it. One common mistake is the seller failing to include a keyword in the title that buyers will search for. A great example is a US seller I heard about who was trying to break into selling on eBay.co.uk by selling low-cost mobile phones. He had plenty of buyers, but he couldn't understand why his items weren't getting similar prices to his competition. It took his British friend to point out that on this side of the Atlantic they aren't often called 'cell phones'.

Another common mistake is misspelling the keywords in the Item Title. One buyer who completed his comic collection by getting his hands on the very first Beano Annual was thrilled that his seller couldn't spell. He got it for about half of what he would have been happy to pay. The seller was miffed that the item hadn't sold for much more. The buyer cheerfully pointed out that other buyers couldn't find

it because the item was described as a 'Beeno Annual'.
Look out for a rare 'Darlek Prop', an 'Agatha Cristy first
edition', 'David Beckam's Signed Boots' or a 'Royal
Dollton Vase'.

• **Wrong category** People are predictable and get into
habits. Some buyers will only check in one category for the
items they want. While most of the items will be located
here, there might be other places where the item can logi-
cally be located. So if a seller puts the item in a less obvious
but nevertheless appropriate category, the chances are that
fewer buyers will be competing to buy it, keeping the price
down.

It's sound advice to check the category an item is listed in
every time you are about to place a bid, just to be sure. I
heard about a guy who thought he'd got himself a real bargain. He was looking for one of those old-fashioned wooden
filing cabinets and was amazed to find one for less than a
tenner with really low postage. Desperate not to let the bargain go, he placed a bid immediately and paid quickly in
case the seller changed their mind. He waited anxiously for
it to arrive but felt like an idiot when it did turn up: it was
four inches tall and meant for a doll's house. If he had
checked the category, he'd have known to expect miniature
furniture that had been photographed in its correspondingly
tiny surroundings rather than in the seller's opulent
Edwardian townhouse.

• **Do the legwork** There is no fast track for finding bargains or a way of searching for items that have been listed
badly. You've just got to hunt them out and second-guess
the other bargain-hunters out there. Not only will you pick
up a few really good bargains, you'll soon know eBay.co.uk
inside out.

Listings Pages

Whether you are browsing or searching for items you will be
presented with a page of listings that will look very much like
this:

Back to Music Overview   Home > All Categories > Music > CDs > **Indie/ Britpop**

All Items	Auctions	Buy It Now

[Indie/ Britpop] [▼] [Search] Refine Search

☐ Search title **and** description

Music: CDs Finder

Format
[Any ▼]

Genre
[Any ▼]

[▼]

Condition
[Any ▼]

Search Keywords
[ ]

[Show Items]

Categories

Indie/ Britpop
- 1970s (24)
- 1980s (518)
- 1990s (5696)
- 2000s (3901)

Search Options

Show items:
◉ United Kingdom
○ Worldwide

Show only:
☐ Items listed with PayPal
☐ Buy It Now items
☐ Items in New Condition
☐ Items listed as lots
☐ Completed listings
☐ Listings
[Starting today ▼]
☐ Items priced
[ ] to [ ]

[Show Items]

Customise options displayed above.

More on eBay

Related Shops
- 24inverness(69)
- Ginger Records(62)
- ARTISANCOMPUTERS (57)
- Bassline 182(38)

See all matching Shops

10109 items found in **Indie/ Britpop**   Add to My Favourite Categories

List View | Picture Gallery   Sort by: [Time: ending soonest ▼]   Customise Display

	Item Title	Price	Bids	Time Left
☐	Return To The Last Chance Saloon - Bluetones (The) (...)	£0.99	-	<1m
☐	Graham Coxon - Rare two track cd!!	£0.99	-	1m
☐	Graham Coxon - Rare one track cd!!	£0.99	-	2m
☐	Everything Must Go - Manic Street Preachers (CD)	£1.99	-	2m
☐	Deftones - Rare one track cd!!	£0.99	2	4m
☐	Hiding Place - Rare four track cd!!	£0.99	-	6m
☐	The Music - Take The Long Road 5 track cd(cd2)	£4.72	7	9m
☐	THE HIVES Main Offender EUROPEAN CD Single Live/ENHANCD	£0.99	1	9m
☐	Deftones -Rare one track cd..!!	£0.99	2	12m
☐	Know Your Enemy - Manic Street Preachers (CD)	£1.99	-	13m
☐	Be Here Now - Oasis (CD 1997)	£1.20	2	13m
☐	MANIC STREET PREACHERS Masses Against The Classes LTD	£0.99	-	14m
☐	Archie Bronson Outfit -Rare three track cd..!!	£0.99	-	14m
☐	KEANE - LIVE AT LONDON & LA	£4.00	-	14m
☐	MCCARTNEY/BEATLES - LIVE AT GLASTONBURY 2004	£4.00	-	15m
☐	PIXIES CARTER USM MEKONS WOLFGANG PRESS ROUGH TRADE CD	£3.99	*Buy It Now*	15m
☐	OASIS - LIVE AT GLASTONBURY 2004	£4.00	-	16m
☐	STARSAILOR LIVE AT GLASTONBURY 2004	£4.00	-	16m
☐	Bonnie Prince Billy -Rare one track cd..!!	£4.20	4	16m
☐	SNOW PATROL - LIVE AT GLASTONBURY 2004	£4.00	1	17m
☐	The Duke Spirit -Rare one track cd..!!	£2.15	6	18m
☐	KEANE LIVE AT GLASTONBURY 2004	£4.00	-	18m
☐	(What's The Story) Morning Glory - Oasis (CD 1995)	£4.10	7	18m
☐	MORRISSEY LIVE AT GLASTONBURY 2004	£4.00	-	18m

A Listings Page shows the items in the category you are browsing or the results from the search you have made. It displays the Titles of the items for sale. They have been crafted by sellers to attract the attention of buyers: they are the short summaries that aim to attract your attention.

Whether you are browsing or searching you can sort the results or narrow them down by using the options on these pages. The results default to 'Time: Ending Soonest', but if you want to change the order of the items you see first you can choose from 'Newly Listed', 'Price: Lowest First' and 'Price: Highest First' by choosing the relevant option under the 'Sort by' tab.

You can also narrow down the results in two ways. First, you can choose the format of the items you see. You automatically see 'All Items', but if you are only interested in Auctions or prefer to buy instantly using Buy It Now, you can opt to see only those items by clicking on the relevant tab.

Choosing a category is also a good way of getting closer to the item you want. By selecting the most relevant category from the list on the lefthand side you will only be shown items listed there.

Sometimes when you are searching or browsing eBay you will also see the Product Finder on the lefthand side of the Listings Pages. This is a useful way of boiling down the results until you find the item you want. The category you are rummaging through will determine the options the Product Finder provides you with. In the DVD category, for instance, you will be able to search the items by Genre and Region. In CDs you can choose to search only albums, EPs or singles, or if you prefer you can select a musical style such as Indie or Rock.

Deciding to Buy an Item

Once you have found an item you like the look of, you will need to decide whether it is exactly what you want and whether the price is right. You'll also need to make sure the delivery and postage costs are suitable for you. These are just the sort of things you would need to do if you were buying from a mail-order catalogue or another ecommerce site.

There is one extra thing you need to do on eBay to make sure that you have a satisfactory and safe purchase: check out the seller. eBay provides buyers with information about sellers that is worth looking at before you take the plunge and place your bid.

Find out More about the Item

If you click on an Item Title when you are browsing or searching eBay you will be taken to the View Item page. This is a page constructed by the seller that tells you about the item for sale. It is your opportunity to find out all about the item and decide whether you want to place a bid.

• **Item details** The top of the View Item page displays the Item Title you've already seen on the Listings Page. The top of the page has all sorts of vital details about how long the listing has to run, how much the bidding currently is and where the seller is located. If the seller has included a photo it will be shown in miniature on the lefthand side. You will also be able to see where the seller is willing to send the item.

There are two other things worth knowing about at the top of the View Item page. Both are on the righthand side. At the top you can see a text link 'Add to watch list in My eBay' and just below you can see the Seller Information Box. These features will be dealt with later.

• **Item description and picture** If you scroll further down the page you'll find the description and most probably a bigger picture. This section is where the seller fully describes the item they have for sale. A good seller will have taken a few moments to provide all the relevant details needed to persuade you to place a bid. Typically you'll find information about the item's condition, contents and anything else the seller wants you to know in the hope of nudging you towards a bid.

• **Postage and payment details** If you like the Item Description and are tempted to place a bid, it's a good idea to check that the postage costs are reasonable and you are happy to cover them. Typically buyers pay for carriage of the item, so you need to keep the additional charges in mind when you are deciding how much to bid. Sellers can detail the cost of postage within the UK and also what it will cost to send the item overseas.

On this part of the View Item page the seller can also include extra details about getting paid and state their Returns Policy if they want.

• **Payment methods accepted** Before you get to the bottom of the page you'll see one last section where the seller makes a quick note of how they are willing to be paid. Make sure you can pay the seller before you bid. A good seller will offer a selection of payment methods to help buyers.

Find out More about the Seller

If you like the item and you want to place a bid, you now have to make sure you like the seller. It only takes a moment and is time well spent.

On the top righthand side of the View Item page you can see the Seller Information Box; this section contains a precis of the Seller's reputation on eBay. For starters you'll see the seller's Feedback score in brackets by the User ID: this is a tally of the Feedback they have received from unique members. Obviously a higher number indicates a greater number of successful trades. But you shouldn't just consider this number in isolation, which is why you can also see what percentage of positive Feedback the seller has received.

The Seller Information Box also tells you when the seller registered with eBay and where they are located. If a seller is located in a different country from the item, you should be a little more cautious.

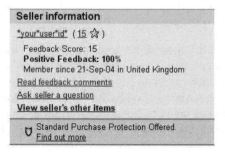

If you want more information from the seller about the item you are looking at, click the 'Ask seller a question' text link.

Feedback

One of eBay's unique strengths, and your most valuable trading tool, is Feedback. Every time you trade on eBay as a buyer or seller you have the right to leave a comment about your trading partner. The comments members leave for each other are public and available for scrutiny by anyone who wants to look. These comments can help you judge whether or not you want to trade with someone.

Think of Feedback as a personal recommendation. When you are looking for a plumber or builder, you will sound out friends and relations for good experiences. eBay Feedback serves exactly the same purpose: it allows you to get the inside information on a seller or buyer from people who have had firsthand dealings with the person in question.

As explained above, the number that appears in brackets beside the User ID of every member is their Feedback score. This number is your at-a-glance gauge of a member's trading history and eBay reputation. It's a useful ready reckoner, but when you are trading on eBay you will want to find out more. eBay provides you with fuller information in the Member Profile.

Member Profile

To access the Member Profile, click on the Feedback number in brackets. A Member Profile gives you a much more detailed insight into a member's trading history on eBay.

You can leave three types of Feedback: positive, negative and neutral. The type of Feedback you leave will depend on the nature of the experience you have with another member. A positive comment adds one to a member's total, a negative deducts one and a neutral leaves the total the same.

On the Member Profile the types of Feedback a member has received are clearly displayed. It will be obvious if a member has received negative comments and what percentage of the member's Feedback has been positive.

You can get a clearer view of a member's Feedback by sorting it depending on whether it was left by a buyer or a seller. You can also choose to take a look at the Feedback that the member has left for other members.

Member Profile: *your*user*id* (16 ☆)

Feedback Score:	16	Recent Ratings:				
Positive Feedback:	100%		Past Month	Past 6 Months	Past 12 Months	Member since: 21-Sep-04 City: United Kingdom
Members who left a positive:	16					▪ ID History
Members who left a negative:	0	⊕ positive	6	16	16	▪ Items for Sale
All positive feedback received:	16	◎ neutral	0	0	0	
		⊖ negative	0	0	0	Contact Member

Learn about what these numbers mean. **Bid Retractions (Past 6 months): 0**

Most importantly, you can view the actual comments others have left. These are the personal views of other members and can be very enlightening. When you are trading on eBay you should always take the time to examine the Member Profile. Mostly you will discover that a member is honest, fair and reliable, but sometimes you will decide that the seller isn't someone you want to do business with.

Inside Information: Buying Safely

Transactions that go awry remain a very, very small percentage of the many hundreds of thousands of successful trades that occur on eBay every day. That isn't to say that some people don't get ripped off, of course; a tiny number do. My point is that you mustn't go around imagining that there are crooks and conmen at every turn.

When you are shopping online generally, being safe is about minimising the risks and behaving sensibly. If you imagine that eBay is a big city, in fact a huge city of more than 100 million people, most of the citizens are completely law-abiding and trustworthy. You need to exercise the same caution you would in a big city you don't know well. There are some shady characters and some dodgy streets, like in any city, that you probably want to avoid after dark. If you do go there you wouldn't wave your camera around, wear expensive jewellery or have your wallet poking out of your back pocket because that's asking for trouble.

When it comes to being safe on eBay, the key is paying safely. Use methods of payment, such as PayPal, that offer you protection and peace of mind. Take the time to research the item and seller and trust your instincts. If you take the precautions, do your research and pay safely, the chances are you'll never have a problem on eBay. There is more on payments later in the book.

5
Placing a Bid

Once you have decided you like the item and the seller, you are ready to place a bid. Placing a bid is very easy, but you can maximise your chances of winning the item by understanding how the eBay bidding system works.

Inside Information:
Why There Are Bargains on eBay

There really are bargains on eBay. I bought my vacuum cleaner on eBay: if I'd bought it in the shops I would have paid £80 and have had to drag it home on the bus. On eBay I paid £50 including delivery direct to my door. I put the £30 I saved towards a handheld digital radio. The model I bought on eBay retails in the shops at £99 and I got mine for £68 all in. Another £30 saved! If I need to buy something, I always make a point of checking out eBay first. I'd be mad not to.

How is this possible? How can sellers on eBay undercut the High Street? There are lots of reasons. It won't surprise you to hear that manufacturers and retailers end up with a lot of stock they can't sell. It could be because they have over-produced, taken returns and seconds, or are pushing a new product that means the old model is now surplus to requirements. There are warehouses full of stuff that shops can't shift. What you might not know is that it costs money to get rid of this stuff. For a business, disposing of unwanted goods is expensive.

eBay offers a way of selling it, so rather than paying to get rid of it they can actually make money. Everyone wins. The manufacturers make something back and the rest of us bag a bargain. As my dad would say, rubbing his hands together like Del Boy, 'Everybody's happy!'

If the manufacturers and wholesalers decide not to sell their overstock on eBay, they might make it available to eBay sellers. I've met loads of eBay sellers who buy their stock from big names and chains. They buy it by the pallet load and often don't know what they are going to get. They break down the pallets and sell the stuff on. They buy it cheap, they keep their overheads low and the savings are passed on to the buyer. Sometimes the box may be scuffed or it's not the latest model. But really, who cares? It's a good bit of kit and you've saved money.

Other businesses sell on eBay because it is extremely cost-effective. They can avoid the huge costs of maintaining a shop or premises in a prime location. For instance, I met one seller who used to run a costly shop in his local town centre. Now he operates from a converted barn in his village. This saves him money, is much more convenient and provides a pleasanter working environment where he need no longer fear the sudden pounce of a traffic warden. eBay can also help sellers cut other operating costs so they can keep their prices low and stay competitive.

And then of course there's everyone else, the individual sellers. Many of these are people who are simply selling things they don't need any more. Often they are merely glad to get something for the item rather than chuck it away or take it to the tip or charity shop. The constant flow of goods means there's always a bargain to be found on eBay. You just need to seek those bargains out.

How Bidding Works

eBay does most of the bidding work for you. You don't need to sit in front of your computer day and night once you have decided to bid: all you need to do is enter the maximum amount you are willing to pay. eBay will then do the bidding on your behalf up to your maximum while you do other things. This is called Proxy Bidding. If other people have placed bids, eBay will ensure that you are the highest bidder for as long as your maximum bid is greater than anyone else's.

Most importantly, eBay won't bid more than is necessary for you to stay ahead of the other bidders. For instance, if you have bid £10.01 for a CD and another bidder has placed a bid of £4.01, eBay won't bid up to your maximum. What it will do is push your bid up to just above the other bidder, making your bid £4.21. If no one else bids on the CD, despite the fact you are willing to bid up to £10.01, your winning bid will only be £4.21.

  • **Bid increments** eBay uses a fixed system of Bid Increments to control bidding. Depending on the price of the item, the bidding will go up according to these fixed Bid Increments:

PRICE	BID INCREMENT
£0.01–1.00	£0.05
£1.01–5.00	£0.20
£5.01–15.00	£0.50
£15.01–60.00	£1.00
£60.01–150.00	£2.00
£150.01–300.00	£5.00
£300.01–600.00	£10.00
£600.01–1,500.00	£20.00
£1,500.01–3,000.00	£50.00
Above £3000.01	£100.00

If yours is the first bid on an item, your bid will be the Starting Price of the item. If you are bidding on an item that already has bids and your bid is higher than the other bidder's maximum bid, then eBay will bid up to the other bidder's maximum plus one increment. If your maximum bid is higher than the other bidder's maximum bid but not a whole increment higher, eBay will automatically bid to your maximum regardless.

• **Proxy bidding** is often a source of confusion to new buyers. In particular, many newbies wonder why they are immediately outbid when they place a bid. Obviously this is because the maximum bid they place isn't as high as the other bidder's maximum. The best way to get to grips with how bidding works is to practise and experiment. If at first you don't seem to be winning auctions, don't worry: find another and just keep on bidding!

How to Place a Bid

To place a bid you can either click on 'Place Bid' at the top of the View Item page or scroll down to the bottom of the page and enter your bid there. You'll need to sign in and confirm the amount you are bidding.

• **Bids are binding** A bid is legally binding. If you aren't serious about buying the item then you shouldn't place a bid. Sellers get narked by people who place bids and don't pay up and if you do it you will most likely earn yourself negative Feedback. Under some circumstances you are permitted to 'Retract a Bid', but if you do it will be noted on your Member Profile. Be warned that other members don't look kindly on members who retract bids. You can 'Retract a Bid' via the link on the Site Map.

• **Getting outbid** If another bidder places a maximum bid greater than yours, you will be outbid. When you are outbid you have the option to raise your maximum and regain the item. You can up your bid in the same way as placing a bid.

Bidding Strategies

Once you have found an item you want to bid on, there are ways of improving your chances of winning that auction. If you have found an item you want at a price you like, then it's very likely that other people will be bidding too. Experienced eBay buyers can sometimes be at an advantage because they know how the eBay bidding system works. You need to formulate a bidding strategy if you're going to be competing against them.

• **Decide your maximum bid and stick to it** The worst mistake a buyer can make is bidding more than they want to pay. Sometimes people can get carried away with their bidding because they want to beat the other bidders and their competitive instinct gets the better of them. Once you have found an item you want to buy, decide the maximum you want to pay for it and stick to that. If the bidding goes higher you can either reassess your bid or wait for another similar item to come up. Don't forget to consider the postage costs when you are deciding your maximum bid. Sometimes when you add in the postage the bargain you wanted to bag doesn't look so attractive.

• **Don't bid round numbers** If the maximum you want to bid is £10, then it is advisable not to bid £10.00 straight. The eBay system will favour a bid of £10.01 or £10.03 over £10. A higher bid, even if the difference is only a penny, will take preference over a lower one. In the event of two bids being equal, the earliest one will take preference. Experienced eBay buyers will always bid a few extra pence.

• **Watch an item** Wise men say only fools rush in. If you spot an item you want to buy and have decided how much you want to bid, it can be worth biding your time if the item has only just started or has a number of days left to run. It's a bit like playing poker: you don't always want to show your hand too soon. By being the first person to bid on an item early on in the listing, you are expressing your interest, which can alert other members or mean that in the long run you are pushing the price up. eBay gives you the opportunity to watch an item (meaning the item is displayed in My eBay and you can keep an eye on it and choose to bid later if you want to). To watch an item simply click the link on the View Item page and the item will be added to your Watch List.

• **Last-minute bidding** For some members the real thrill of buying on eBay is waiting for the last minute and bidding in the dying seconds in the hope of outwitting other potential buyers and bagging a bargain. Bidding in the last minutes of a listing is called 'sniping' by eBay regulars, who find it an exciting way of using the site.

Inside Information: Sniping

> *Sniping is a controversial issue for many members of eBay and one of those topics that is guaranteed to get a robust discussion going on the Chat Boards. Snipers believe that keeping their bid secret until the last minute means that the price is kept low and they can beat the other bidders by the smallest amount necessary. The end of a listing on eBay is non-negotiable and if a bid is received in the final moments, there isn't time for anyone else to bid even if they are willing to bid more than the sniper.*

> *Snipers believe that the highest bid should win and they can get the items they want at the price they like. But for the people who are outbid it can seem desperately unfair to be robbed of an item at the last minute by a matter of pence, especially if they were willing to pay more. The options are clear. Either become a sniper, or bid your maximum bid and be happy to accept that you didn't want to pay more even when you are outbid at the last minute.*

Using Buy It Now

Buying on eBay doesn't need to be simply about bidding and using the auction format. You can also buy instantly at a fixed price by using Buy It Now. Clicking 'Buy It Now' ends the listing immediately and the item is yours. The Buy It Now price is determined by the seller and you can either take it or leave it.

This option can be seen on its own on pure fixed-price items or it can be added by the seller to any auction item. If you see an auction item with Buy It Now, you have the choice to bid or purchase the item instantly. If you want to bid, just treat the item as a normal auction item. Once you have placed a bid, the Buy It Now option will disappear. If you would rather use Buy It Now because you like the fixed price, click the 'Buy It Now' button and you can buy the item instantly.

Keeping Track of Your Buying Activities

Once you have placed a few bids you'll know that eBay can get addictive: it's difficult to keep away from your computer because you want to make sure you are still the highest bidder. For ease eBay organises the details of your buying activities in a special section called My eBay.

My eBay

My eBay is a personalised summary of your trading activities. You can see at a glance the items you are bidding on, auctions you have won and those that you have bid on but not won. You can access My eBay by clicking on the 'My eBay' link in the Navigation Bar. You will need to sign in using your User ID and password.

> • **Your summary** When you log in to My eBay you will be taken to the Summary page, which gives you a selection of the most important information you can find in My eBay. At the top, eBay provides reminders about items you need to pay for. A bit further down the page you can see news from eBay in the 'Latest Announcements' section. If eBay is launching a new feature, changing a policy or holding a Free Listing Day, it will tell the community about it here.

If you want to go to specific trading information, you can navigate through My eBay by using the links on the lefthand side of the page.

• **Your buying information** As a buyer all the information you need to keep tabs on your activities can be found by clicking on the 'All Buying' link. In this section of My eBay you can see what you have bid on, whether you are the highest bidder and what you need to pay for. My eBay is a very intuitive and well-organised part of eBay. If you want to find out what a symbol or icon means, just position your mouse pointer over it and some explanatory text will pop up. If you want to find out where a link goes, simply click on it. You can always go back to where you started by clicking the 'Back' button on your browser.

• **Save your favourites** As a buyer there is a second useful section of My eBay that you can use to make your trading easier. If you click on the 'All Favourites' link, you'll find a great resource to help you store information about your favourite searches, sellers and categories.

• **Customise My eBay** eBay offers you the opportunity to customise how the information in My eBay is displayed. Within each section you can use the double arrow icons to change the order in which the information appears. If you want something nearer the top you can use the up arrows, and if you aren't as interested in something you can move it towards the bottom of the page. You can organise My eBay to your liking by clicking on the 'Customise' link at the top right of the page.

• **Information for sellers** As you develop your eBay trading and move on to becoming a seller, you'll find that My eBay is indispensable. When you are a buyer it helps you organise your purchases by giving you information on what you have bought and for how much. For a seller My eBay is the nerve centre of activity: it lets you know how the bidding is going on items you are selling, which of your buyers have paid and which of your sales you have despatched.

Buying from Sellers in Other Countries

One of eBay's greatest attractions is the opportunity it opens up for buying items from other countries. eBay has established websites in more than 30 countries and your eBay.co.uk registration allows you to buy on any eBay site just as you would in the UK.

There are obvious benefits to buying items from abroad. Sometimes an item will be considerably cheaper than in Britain. Electronic accessories are often much cheaper when purchased from the US. Designer clothing is much cheaper in Italy. eBay also makes it easier to buy items from abroad that simply aren't available in the UK. Collectables, stamps, books, magazines, comics and records that would otherwise be unobtainable can be snapped up with ease.

Buying from abroad shouldn't be a chore if you follow a few simple steps:

- **Make sure the seller will send the item to the UK** If you are searching for items on eBay.co.uk and what you want shows up as located elsewhere in the world, the chances are that the seller will send the item to the UK. To double-check, sellers indicate where they are willing to send the item to on the View Item page. If a seller doesn't say they are willing to ship to the UK but you are very keen on the item, you could ask the seller if they would make an exception. With the reassurance that you are keen and able to complete the transaction, they might broaden their horizons.

- **Make sure you can communicate with the seller** If you are buying from a seller in the US, Canada or Australia, language won't be an issue. However, with other European countries and sellers in Asia or South America it can be a barrier. Many overseas sellers do indicate that they are willing to conduct the sale in English, but if it isn't clear it is best to contact the seller to ensure you can communicate. Obviously, if you speak their language, trading won't be a problem.

- **Make sure you can pay** For international traders the number one source of problems is payment. Despite modern technology, paying for items across borders can still be time-consuming, expensive and slow. So if you do bid on an item located overseas, make sure you can meet the seller's payment terms.

If the seller accepts PayPal then there won't be a problem because you can pay them with speed and ease. If they don't accept PayPal you will find other options on the View Item page. Remember, money orders and cheques sent overseas can attract high conversion fees and many sellers will expect you to meet those costs. If you need to send small amounts of money overseas, cash can be the easiest if not the safest option.

• **Make sure the postage costs are acceptable** International postage can be expensive so to avoid a nasty shock, make sure you have an idea of the postage costs before bidding. Some sellers note international rates in the item description. If you are in any doubt, send the seller an email and ask for an estimate before you bid. If you aren't in a hurry to receive the item remember that surface mail is much cheaper than air mail.

• **And don't forget Customs** Items sent to the UK from outside the European Union are sometimes liable to customs charges. Not every parcel is stopped and assessed, but if it is and a charge is levied then it will be your responsibility to pay it. You should bear this in mind when you bid. You can find full details on the Customs and Excise website: www.hmce.gov.uk.

6

Completing Your Purchase

Once you have successfully bought an item you will have to pay the seller, receive the item and leave the seller Feedback. It's important that you pay swiftly and work with the seller so you can get your hands on the item as quickly as possible.

Paying the Seller

Many new members are confused about paying for their first purchase. Paying for an item needn't be a problem as long as you have taken the time to examine the payment methods the seller is willing to accept on the View Item page. If the seller is willing to accept a number of payment methods, you can choose the one that suits you best. Obviously, the quicker the seller has the payment the quicker they will despatch the goods.

Checkout

The Checkout process helps you pay quickly and sends the seller your delivery details at the same time. There are two ways to enter Checkout. The first is via My eBay. By clicking on the Item Title in the 'Items I've Won' section of My eBay, you will be taken to the View Item page. After the Listing has ended the page looks slightly different from when you were bidding. Near the top of the page you will see a 'Pay Now' button. Just click on it and you will be guided through the payment process. You will be able to choose the payment method you want to use, enter your address so it's sent to the seller, and if you want to pay by cheque you will receive the seller's address so you know where to send it. You will also be sent an email with all these details for your reference.

You can also access Checkout via the automatic email that eBay sends you when you have won an auction. You can get started by clicking on the 'Pay Now' button in the email.

The first time you go through the Checkout is the most time consuming. Every time you use Checkout in future will be quicker because eBay will store your address so you won't need to add it again and again. If you want to add multiple addresses for your convenience, you can.

How will I know how much I need to pay?

The Checkout facility tots up the price plus the postage automatically and will tell you how much you have to pay.

If you are in any doubt about the postage costs or want to clarify anything with the seller, you are best advised to contact them directly. At the end of the Listing you will receive an email from eBay informing you that you have successfully purchased the item. This email will include the seller's email address for your reference.

PayPal

On many eBay listings you will see that PayPal is offered as a payment option. PayPal is a swift and easy way of paying your seller online using your credit or debit card. It is popular with many eBay buyers because you can pay instantly, but your card details are kept secure and confidential from the seller. In fact, PayPal has proved so popular with buyers and sellers that eBay bought the company in 2002 so that the two organisations' services could be effectively integrated.

What do I need to join PayPal?

Joining PayPal is very simple. All you require is a credit or debit card and an email address. For ease, it's best to use the same email address you used to register with eBay. PayPal accepts Visa, MasterCard, Maestro, American Express, Switch and Solo cards. To register go to www.paypal.co.uk.

Once you have registered with PayPal you can bid on
eBay listings displaying the PayPal logo safe in the knowledge
that you will be able to pay quickly and easily if you win the
item.

How do I pay with PayPal?

If you have won an item from a seller who accepts PayPal, the
easiest way to pay for the item is by using eBay's Checkout
facility. If you use PayPal the seller will instantly know you have
paid because it will show in their My eBay. As you are guided
through Checkout you will be asked to choose how you want to
pay. By choosing PayPal, you will be automatically taken to the
PayPal site to complete your payment.

Regardless of how you are paying, if you are in any doubt,
it's always best to contact the seller directly. If you want to pay
with PayPal, the seller can then send you an invoice via email.

What are the benefits of PayPal for buyers?

The greatest benefit of using PayPal is speed. When you send a
PayPal payment the seller has the funds immediately and can
safely send the item straight away. Without PayPal you would
have to send a cheque, wait for the seller to receive it and then
wait for it to clear. PayPal speeds up the buying process and
doesn't cost buyers anything.

If you use PayPal to pay for an eBay purchase you can also
enjoy greater protection and peace of mind. PayPal is a trackable
payment method, so you can be reassured that you aren't sending
your payment into the blue never to be seen again. If you pay by
PayPal you can also enjoy the benefits of the PayPal Buyer
Protection Programme if the seller is eligible.

PayPal is also terrific for international trading. You can use
your British debit card or credit card to pay sellers from all over
the world and PayPal takes care of the currency conversion.

Inside Information:
Why PayPal Is Bloody Marvellous

*The beauty of PayPal is security. You can pay individuals
using a debit or credit card without having to reveal your
personal details to people you don't know. PayPal keeps
your details safe, the seller gets paid immediately and*

everybody's happy. I just wish I could use PayPal for more mundane things like the phone bill and council tax.

The security is reassuring, but I also love the speed and convenience. If I bid and win or use Buy It Now I like to pay immediately. Good sellers despatch the item a day or two later and another day or so after that I have the item I bought. Often buying on eBay is quicker than ordering online with other companies because sellers take such a pride in shipping items speedily.

Unless the item is really rare and I have no choice, I won't bid on an item if the seller doesn't take PayPal. I just can't be bothered with the hassle of digging out my chequebook, writing a note, finding an envelope, applying a stamp and putting it in the post. It'll take a day or two (at least) and then I have to wait for the seller to bank it and let it clear. If I'm lucky my purchase will turn up a week or so later.

What amazes me is that there are sellers out there who won't take PayPal. What are they thinking? It could save them time: they could turn their sales round much more quickly and be saved many trips to the bank. And of course there are all those people who send a cheque without including a note so you have to spend time working out who the cheque is actually from. Moreover, by not taking PayPal, they are losing sales. It's not just me who avoids sellers who don't take PayPal: I talk to members all the time who 'can't be bothered' when it comes to writing a cheque or indeed have bank accounts that don't use chequebooks.

For international trading it is almost impossible to imagine life without PayPal. When I started buying and selling on eBay in 1999, before PayPal was available to Brits, sending and receiving money to and from eBay members overseas was expensive, time consuming and very unsafe. Many of the buyers were in the States. The options for receiving payment were limited. International Money Orders were safe and pretty convenient, but the charges my bank levied to convert them were exorbitant. My buyers were as reluctant to cover the conversion costs as I was. Often we compromised and they sent dollars in cash and we all hoped for the best. When I had accrued a small stack of dollars I would convert them to sterling. Or I would use them to buy things from American sellers and send them back over the Atlantic. It was ludicrous.

Then PayPal came along. You received the funds immediately, they were safe from thieving hands and converted into sterling. It totally transformed international trading on eBay. I love PayPal and I don't care what anyone says: I won't go back to the bad old days.

Other Payment Methods

So by far the easiest way to pay your seller is to use PayPal, which is instant and free to buyers. However, not all sellers are willing to accept PayPal, so sometimes you may need to use another method.

You can find the payment methods that sellers are willing to accept on the View Item page. Always check that you can use a method acceptable to the seller before you bid.

• **Cheques and postal orders** Within the UK it is simple to send a cheque or postal order to your seller. When you do so, don't forget to include a note with your payment so the seller knows who it is from. Include your email address, User ID and the item number.

• **Other online methods** For sending money to sellers in the UK there are several online services available favoured by some sellers. None is as prevalent as PayPal and none is currently particularly useful for sending money abroad, but some sellers will accept them. The most popular of these services are Nochex and Fastpay.

• **Cash** Some sellers are happy to accept cash as long as it is sent at the buyer's risk. Remember that cash is uninsurable in the post, so even if it is the only option it isn't advisable. Certainly, never ever send large amounts of cash and if you do opt to send cash always disguise it well. Also remember that eBay's protection programmes won't apply if you pay by cash.

• **Bank transfer** Some sellers like to be paid directly into their bank account by bank transfer. Many buyers are uncomfortable with this option and if you are in any doubt about the seller this method should be avoided. There is

nothing wrong with paying by bank transfer. Just never do it
internationally and absolutely don't use it for high-value
items.

International Payment Methods

For ease, security and peace of mind your best method for paying
a seller overseas is PayPal. However, if the seller doesn't accept
PayPal you do have other options. Some sellers will accept payment in their local currency in cash. Obviously for small amounts
this can be acceptable (even though you will have to meet the
conversion costs too), but for more expensive items it is too much
of a risk. International Money Orders are available from your
bank but they can cost you money to obtain and the seller may
face further charges to cash them; you will most likely be
expected to meet these conversion costs too.

When paying internationally you need to be careful of any
means of payment that you cannot track. Bank transfers overseas
can be exploited by unscrupulous people, as can some Western
Union services. eBay recommends that you use PayPal for international purchases.

Receiving the Item

As with any distance-buying experience, the most frustrating
aspect is waiting for the item to arrive. Many eBay members say
that waiting for the delivery is like waiting for a birthday gift or
exam results.

Many more times than not, your item will arrive swiftly and
in exactly the condition you expect. Sometimes the item will be
even better than described, which is why you often see 'Item
better than expected' in Feedback comments. If you are happy
with the item when it arrives you can go and leave the seller positive Feedback immediately. Sometimes, however, your buying
experience might be less than perfect.

What if My Item Isn't What I Expected?

The vast majority of sellers understand how eBay works and describe their items honestly. Nevertheless sometimes the items might have been misrepresented, deliberately or accidentally, so you should contact the seller and tell them. eBay will take action against sellers who misdescribe the items they are selling. If a seller misdescribes an item and won't offer you recompense when you inform them, you should inform eBay via the webform in the Help section.

If the item was damaged in the post, you should contact the seller. The cover you can expect will depend on the delivery method: if you opted for insured post you will have extra cover. You will need to work with the seller to make a claim. If the damage was a result of poor packaging, then you have good reason to expect the seller to see you right.

What if My Purchase Doesn't Arrive?

If your item doesn't arrive at all you should follow these steps:

- **Contact the seller** The first thing you should always do if you haven't received the item in good time is to get in touch with the seller. A polite and friendly enquiry will usually get an apologetic reply. In the first instance be patient; don't forget that many sellers are busy people and they may simply have forgotten to send the item. In other cases the Royal Mail may just have let them down and it might be lost in the post. You should always try to work the problem out with the seller if you can.

- **Contact eBay** If you have sent the money to the seller, contacted them to chase your purchase up and still not received the item, then you should contact eBay. They will chase up the seller on your behalf and you won't be surprised to hear how quickly a tardy seller swings into action when threatened with suspension from eBay. You can report a seller via the 'Help' link in the Navigation Bar.

Buyer Protection Programmes

If your purchase fails to arrive and your seller is uncooperative, then you may need to resort to using one of the Buyer Protection Programmes offered by eBay or PayPal. Most items for sale on eBay are protected under one of two schemes. To ensure that an item is covered you need to check out the Seller Information Box on the View Item page.

- **PayPal Buyer Protection** If an item is covered by PayPal Buyer Protection you will see a PayPal logo and the text 'PayPal Buyer Protection' in the Seller Information Box. The PayPal Programme will cover you for purchases up to a total value of £500 as long as the seller and the item are eligible.

- **eBay Buyer Protection** eBay's purchase protection is available on just about every eBay item. You are covered up to a total of £120 minus a £15 administration fee. If you are covered this text is visible in the Seller Information Box: Standard Buyer Protection Offered.

- **Exclusions** Both programmes have some exclusions that you should be aware of before you place your bid. Only 'tangible' items are covered. Items such as ebooks, information or software downloads are not covered. For the PayPal programme you obviously need to pay for the item with PayPal. Under the eBay programme you are not eligible if you have paid using cash or a wire transfer service such as Western Union or Moneygram. You must also make your claim within a specified time after the listing has ended.

- **Extra protection** If the item you are purchasing is more expensive than the coverage offered by the Protection Programmes you should consider getting extra protection. A reputable escrow service might be the appropriate option (there is more on this later in the book).

You can find out further details about the Buyer Protection Programmes and make a claim via this page:

http://pages.ebay.co.uk/help/confidence/purchase-protection.html

Leaving Feedback

By this stage you will be aware of the value of Feedback as a trading tool: it's how eBay members can judge the reputation of others in an honest way based on other people's experiences.

This is why it is important to leave Feedback when you have received your purchase. Your experience as a buyer will be invaluable to other members who are trying to trade successfully. Your positive Feedback will encourage others to bid. Your negative Feedback may warn them off.

Feedback is vital to sellers. A good seller takes pride in receiving glowing Feedback. For sellers, better Feedback means better sales and most like to guard their eBay reputation jealously. Negative Feedback can be a warning to sellers that their performance isn't up to scratch and they need to reassess their activities. Negative Feedback also serves as a warning to eBay. A seller with negative Feedback can warrant investigation and perhaps suspension from the site.

How Do I Leave Feedback?

The easiest way to leave Feedback is to use the Feedback link in My eBay. Click on the My eBay link in the Navigation Bar and sign in. Once you are in My eBay there is a 'Feedback' link on the lefthand side and if you click on that you will be taken to a list of all the Feedback you have to leave. You can then opt to leave a Feedback comment by clicking the 'Leave Feedback' link.

Which Type of Feedback Should I Leave?

The type of Feedback you leave will depend on your experience with the seller. Positive Feedback should be left if you are very satisfied with the transaction, happy with your item and pleased with the service you received. If you are not entirely satisfied but found the service and item acceptable, you might want to leave neutral Feedback. Many sellers will be very unhappy to receive a neutral: it is considered to be almost as bad as a negative. So if you are thinking about leaving neutral Feedback you might want to contact the seller before you do, so they understand why you want to leave a neutral and have a chance to remedy any problems you feel have occurred.

Fact: Jayandmarie are the eBay sellers with the most Feedback. Search for their User ID to see how much they currently have.

Negative Feedback Is a Last Resort

Leaving negative Feedback is a serious business, so you need to be sure that it is the right thing to do. You also need to give the seller a chance to change your mind. Politely email the seller and explain why you are dissatisfied. Keep your email calm and factual and try to outline your thoughts clearly so they can understand exactly why you are dissatisfied. Don't forget that sometimes an email can seem very cold and the words can be easily misunderstood. A problem may be more easily resolved by giving the seller a call.

If you have contacted the seller and you are unable to resolve the problem between you, then you are clear to leave negative Feedback. Take a few moments to decide what it is you want to say, and don't resort to personal insults or vitriolic comments.

Don't forget that other members can see the Feedback you have left. It can damage your eBay reputation if you look like the kind of member who leaves negative Feedback in haste and anger. As a buyer sellers might cancel your bids, and as a seller it could cost you sales.

Make Sure Your Feedback Comments Are Useful

Feedback is about helping other people. On one level by leaving Feedback you are building your own eBay reputation by encouraging reciprocation. But the major value of Feedback lies in what you are offering to the community as a whole. By leaving positive, negative or neutral Feedback you are telling other eBay members about your trading experience. Your comments will help them make successful trading decisions. Your duty as an eBay member is to be honest and helpful. Make sure that the comments you leave, regardless of whether they are good or bad, help other people when they are looking at them. Be factual and objective and relate them directly to your experience.

Feedback Cannot Be Retracted

Only in the rarest of circumstances will eBay totally remove a Feedback comment. So if you say something in Feedback you should expect it to remain part of the other member's Profile forever. This is one reason why you should be cautious and never leave Feedback in the heat of the moment, however tempting it might feel to get your revenge. If you do leave a comment mistakenly you have one option: Mutual Feedback Withdrawal. You can take this path if you and your trading partner both decide that the Feedback you have left each other is no longer appropriate. The Feedback will be removed from the rating, but the comments will both remain. The Member Profile will indicate that a Feedback has been mutually withdrawn.

Feedback Isn't Compulsory

Sometimes you'll leave Feedback and it won't be reciprocated. This is an unfortunate fact of eBay life. If you have left positive Feedback for another member and have not received it in return, you should feel free to drop the other member an email and ask them to reciprocate. Obviously approach them politely, tell them that you'd really appreciate the boost to your rating and nine times out of ten they will return the favour. But if you ask and they don't, while it is obviously annoying, there isn't much you can do. And obviously if you keep on pestering them demanding Feedback, they might even retaliate with a negative.

Fact: More than one million Feedback comments are left every day. Two billion have been left since eBay began.

7

Finding Help on eBay

You'll remember that the idea of getting to know eBay as a buyer was to help you when you become a seller. Getting the hang of using eBay's own Help systems before you start selling is also a very good idea. This way, when you need to find something out in a hurry later, you'll be able to keep your swearing to a minimum.

Buying and selling on eBay is a different experience every time you do it. You might have sold a dozen CDs, but you might never have sent one to South Africa. Most problems are easily solved, but for those that aren't you'll need to find help. eBay knows this and provides a Help system to support traders. If you get stuck you can contact the Customer Support team. For specialist advice on eBay you can also get in touch with the experts: the eBay community. After all, the chances are that someone has faced the same problem before.

Using the Help Section

On the Navigation Bar at the top of nearly every eBay page you can see a link to 'Help'. This link gives you access to eBay's dedicated Help pages. There are hundreds and hundreds of pages containing information and advice on all aspects of trading on the site. Whether you want to know about selling pet food, advice on setting a safe password or information about payment methods, you'll find it here.

How Do I Find the Information I Want?

There are three ways of finding the information you need. You can browse for the information by clicking on the topic you want on the Help front page. If you wanted information about selling, you would click on the selling link and be offered a further list of subtopics. You can keep clicking on the links until you get the page you want. You can also search the Help section to find the information you need in the same way you would search eBay for an item you wanted to buy.

Simply enter a search term relevant to the information you want and click 'Search'. So if you want details about eBay fees you would search for 'fees'. Any relevant Help pages that exist will be listed and you can browse them for the information you want. You can also browse the Help pages by using the A–Z list on the lefthand side.

What if I Can't Find the Information I Need?

With so much information available and so many questions you might want answered, it is possible that you won't be able to find the answer or that it might not even be included in the Help pages. If you can't find the information you require you will need to contact Customer Support or try out the Community Help Boards.

Contacting Customer Support

eBay has Customer Support centres in several countries around the world, including Ireland, Canada and Germany.

How Do I Contact eBay's Customer Support?

You can contact Customer Support in two ways. First, if you are on an eBay Help page and you can't find the answer you want on that page, there will be a link at the bottom to 'Ask a question'.

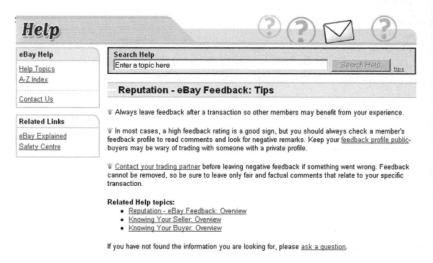

You will be required to sign in and type your query into a text box. Your enquiry will then be sent to Customer Support. Typically you will receive an email back within 24 to 48 hours.

You can also contact Customer Support via the webform, which can be accessed from the lefthand side of the help pages. Simply click on 'Contact Us'. On the webform you have to choose the topic of your query from the list available and then fill in the details and send it to Customer Support.

> • **What should I include in my query?** It is very important that you give the Customer Support representative as much information as possible to help them to provide a relevant and full answer. Obviously include your User ID and if appropriate include the User ID of the person you are trading with. It is always handy to include the item number if your query relates to a specific transaction. Basically include all the important information relating to the transaction.

> Keep your query brief and factual and try to be clear about what you are asking. You might feel angry or upset about a transaction that has gone wrong, but it won't be very useful if you write a long tirade. Just stick to the facts and your chances of getting a swift, correct answer will be higher.

> • **Reporting violations** If you find an item that is against eBay's rules or you need to report a dodgy buyer or seller, you can also do it via the Help area. You can report the item or trader via the relevant Help page or the webform.

> The most effective way of keeping the eBay marketplace safe and pleasant is to report infringing items and sellers when you spot them. eBay will take action if it receives a report.

Community Help Boards

As discussed before, eBay's community is a unique feature that distinguishes it from other online companies like Amazon or traditional old-style companies. The eBay community comprises all the buyers and sellers who use the site. eBay provides Discussion Boards so that community members can discuss their trading, meet friends and enjoy themselves. All registered members can use the Discussion Boards and they offer a unique opportunity to get help from other buyers and sellers.

• **Aren't chat boards just for weirdos?** Some chat boards do have a bad reputation, but the ones on eBay are unusually diverse and friendly. The people who use them are just normal buyers and sellers who enjoy the community atmosphere and being sociable with other people. eBay users become very passionate about their trading and like to talk about their successes and frustrations. eBay offers a common, shared experience, but the boards are not just restricted to eBay-related chat.

• **What are the benefits of using the Discussion Boards?** Sometimes the best person to get help from is someone who understands exactly what you are experiencing. You can find these people on the Discussion Boards. If you are having trouble with a seller, eBay can give general advice about communicating with them or about filing an alert for a buyer who hasn't coughed up. But if you want firsthand experience from other sellers and buyers, the best people to ask are those who might have faced the same issue before. Other eBay members can give you personal insights and candid, opinionated responses.

Many eBay members take a real pride in offering help to less experienced traders. They are very keen to give quick and factual replies about all aspects of eBay trading as well as tips and hints. Think of the Discussion Boards as *the* place to get insider knowledge.

• **Where are the Discussion Boards?** You can find the discussion boards by clicking 'Community' on the Navigation Bar. There are boards for general chat like 'The Round Table' or the 'The Nag's Head'. For trading advice try the 'New to Selling', 'International Trading Help' or 'Community Question and Answer' boards. For PayPal queries or postage questions go to the 'Payments and Postage' board. There is also a dedicated board for new members called the 'New to eBay Help Board', which is an ideal place to start if you have a query.

Announcement Board and System Status Board

One important way that eBay communicates with the buyers and sellers who use the site is via the Announcement Board. Think of this as eBay's official noticeboard for members. If there is a change in a policy or an enhancement to the website on its way, eBay will announce it on the Announcement Board. Also, if there has been a problem with the website eBay will often note it here and inform members of any refunds that are due. The Announcement Board on eBay.co.uk publishes information specific to UK traders.

You should try to keep an eye on the Announcement Board. It is regularly updated and the more you use eBay the more invaluable the information will become. You can also see a digest of recent announcements on the Summary page of My eBay.

The System Status Board should be your first stop if there is an issue or problem with the site. Inevitably with a website the size of eBay, with so many different functions and features, there are sometimes problems. If there is an outage or problem eBay will record it on the System Status Board.

You can access the Announcement Board and System Status Board by clicking on the Community link in the Navigation Bar.

Finding Help on PayPal

Just like eBay, PayPal has a comprehensive Help section for you to refer to if you get stuck. You can access it by going to the PayPal homepage: www.paypal.co.uk.

In the top right corner you will see a text link, 'Help'. Click on it and you will be taken to the Help Centre.

You have three ways to find the information you want. PayPal lists the questions most people ask on this page, so the chances are that a simple query might be addressed there. If it isn't, check out the categories on the lefthand side and navigate down to the topic you want. You can also search PayPal's Help resources using the Search Box on this page in the same way you would search eBay's Help.

Help Centre

Categories
📂 Top Questions
📁 Getting Started
📁 Account Basics
📁 Making Payments
📁 Tracking Payments
📁 Withdrawing Funds
📁 Adding Funds
📁 Protection Policies
📁 Auctions & Logos
📁 Seller Tools
📁 Features

Still having trouble?
Contact Us

Search: Got a question? Find your answer fast.

| Enter your question here | Search |

(Example: "Can I add another email address?")   Search Tips

Top Questions

Q I paid through PayPal without opening an account. Can I sign up now?

Q What can I do to avoid fraudulent sellers?

Q How do I specify a return URL on my website?

Q What are the advantages of using PayPal for my online website payments?

Q Does it cost money to sign up for PayPal?

Q What is the Receipt ID for?

Q How do I sign up?

Q Which PayPal account type is right for me?

Q Is PayPal secure?

Q Why is my PayPal account balance negative?

Q Do I need a PayPal account to pay my seller?

Contacting PayPal Customer Support

You can contact PayPal's Customer Support team via this page by clicking the 'Contact Us' link on the lefthand side at the bottom of the list of categories. You can also contact PayPal via email or by telephone during business hours at the national rate.

PART II

SELLING ON eBAY

8
Selling Your First Item

Once you are a competent buyer on eBay, with a clutch of positive Feedback beside your User ID, you will want to start selling. Selling on eBay can be a great way to make money and many sellers say that once they have sold their first item they become addicted to the thrill of watching the bids on their listing mount up. Many people are surprised by the amounts their items get compared to what they might have reached in the local paper or at a car boot sale. There are so many buyers on eBay that there is a much better chance of finding people who will pay a good price to get their hands on the junk gathering dust in your attic.

Embarking on anything new can be nerve-wracking and selling your first item on eBay can feel like a daunting experience. But don't be worried: selling on eBay is a straightforward and easy process.

This chapter will show you how to register as a seller and list your first item on eBay using the traditional auction-style bidding format.

Inside Information:
My Most Memorable Sale

The most memorable sale I ever made on eBay wasn't the most lucrative. In fact it was a 78 rpm record that I got just about a fiver for. But the reasons the buyer bought it and the delight he so evidently took from finally getting his hands on the record make it stand out for me.

I'd bought a box of 78s on eBay for a quid with the express purpose of splitting the lot and selling them individually. There were more than a hundred of them and I'd got them for a steal because the lady who was selling them hadn't put much effort into the listing. She didn't live far away and when I went to collect them and had a quick look through the box I was certain there were some gems in there.

One record in particular looked interesting. It had a yellow HMV label on it and was marked 'Private Recording'. I listed it along with the others and fully expected it to make a bundle. It didn't, but some of the others got really excellent prices and I got a huge return on my £1 investment.

The guy who bought the yellow label got in touch quickly and was very keen to come and collect the record. He lived nearby and I agreed that he could stop by and collect it in person. When he arrived he was visibly thrilled to finally find the record he had been seeking for decades. The pianist on the record was his grandfather and to his knowledge there were only two other copies in the world. One was in a university archive in the US. The other was in the British National Sound Archives, and was broken. He now had the third, thanks to me and eBay. It makes me smile every time I think of the story.

Preparing to Sell

As the old saying goes, 'failing to prepare is preparing to fail', and on eBay it couldn't be more true. If you sit down to sell your first item in a spare five minutes without any preparation, the chances are that you won't do it justice and you won't sell it successfully. By taking the time to create your first listing you will not only have one successful sale under your belt but you will also have the knowledge to create successful listings again and again.

• **Choose the item you want to sell** For your first sale don't be too ambitious. Consider it a learning experience that will act as a springboard for your later sales. You may be longing to sell your late Uncle Monty's Victorian grandfather clock or desperate to get rid of those ultra-valuable Ming vases, but try to be patient. Make it easy for yourself and sell something that is simple to list and send. Starting with CDs, DVDs, videos, books and collectables is a good way to ease yourself into eBay selling. Once you have a few successful sales behind you, you will be better placed to make a real success of the big-ticket items.

• **Use your experience as a buyer** Take advantage of the wealth of eBay experience you already have to help you as you start out as a seller. You know what attracted you to the items you bought and what inspired you to trust the sellers you bought from. Perhaps it was their detailed description, the clear photographs or the reasonable postage costs laid out in advance. If you were attracted by certain qualities in a listing then other people will be too. If you think like a buyer when you are selling, you can't go far wrong.

• **Emulate the experts** The resources you have at your disposal as you embark on being a seller include other established sellers. Tap their experience and use it to your advantage. Find a seller you like or admire who is selling the sort of things you want to sell and emulate their style. Ask yourself what they are doing right and why their listings are successful. Use their listings as a model for your own. But be warned that copying descriptions and pictures directly from other listings isn't looked on kindly by other sellers or by eBay.

• **Persevere** If at first you don't succeed, try again. Don't be disheartened if your first item doesn't sell. There can be all sorts of reasons why an item doesn't find a buyer, and it's not always your fault. Look on your first listing as a chance to experiment and gain vital experience. And remember that if the item doesn't sell the first time, eBay gives you a second chance by offering a free relisting. If it sells the second time, eBay will credit one lot of listing fees.

Create a Seller's Account

Before you can list your first item you will need to create a Seller's Account. You fill in an online form and provide information that verifies you are who you say you are. eBay requires sellers to provide additional verification in order to maintain the website as a safe trading environment. It will keep your information entirely secure, so there is no need to worry about submitting your personal details.

When you sit down to create your Seller's Account make sure you have the following close to hand:

• **A credit or debit card** You can choose to use a Visa or MasterCard credit card or a Switch or Solo debit card. You cannot use a Visa debit card to register a Seller's Account.

• **A statement that corresponds to the debit or credit card** You will need to enter the postal address relating to the credit or debit card you use. It's best to have the bill to hand so you can enter the information accurately. If the address you enter doesn't match the one on the bill, eBay will reject your attempts to register a Seller's Account.

• **Bank account details** To confirm your identity, eBay requires you to enter your bank account details. You will need the name of your bank, your branch sort code number and your account number.

Tips: Creating a Seller's Account

If you don't have a credit or debit card of your own you can use someone else's card as long as you have their permission. Remember, the card will not be charged to pay your eBay fees unless you choose.

You may have already provided credit or debit card information when you registered if you used an anonymous email address. It might seem odd that you need to provide your card details again, but it is necessary.

Primarily, the information provided here is for verification purposes. At the end of the online form you will have to choose whether you will use your credit card details for your payments or if you will establish a direct debit instead. There is no fee for setting up a Seller's Account.

Enter Seller Registration

Once you have all the details to hand you can get started with Seller Registration. Click 'Sell' in the Navigation Bar on the eBay.co.uk homepage and on the Sell Hub you will need to click 'Sell My Item' and sign in again.

• **Verify your address** The first step is to verify the information that eBay already has about you. Make sure eBay has a valid contact address and telephone number for you.

Once you have double-checked that the details are correct, click 'Continue' at the bottom of the page to go to the next page. If any of the details on the page are incomplete, you will be prompted to correct them before you can continue.

• **Provide credit or debit card information** As mentioned, you will now have to provide details of a credit or debit card. All the information eBay requires can be found on the card you are using. Some of the boxes on the form are marked 'if available', so if they are not applicable to your card type you don't need to fill them in.

You will also need to provide the relevant address associated with the card you are using. Take care when entering the address and the other information, because if the details are incorrect eBay will refuse your attempt to create a Seller's Account, as discussed above.

If you are entering credit card details you will also need to provide your Card Verification Number. You can find this printed on the signature strip on the reverse of your card. You only need to enter the last three digits. Once you have entered all your details click the 'Continue' button.

• **Provide bank account details** You will now need to provide your bank account details. Enter your name, the name of your bank, and your account number and sort code. All this information can be found on a bank statement, your bank card or cheque. As before, once all this information has been entered, click 'Continue' to proceed to the next page.

• **Choose how to pay your eBay fees** Many people find this section the most confusing. You are required to choose a payment method for your eBay selling fees using the information you have provided. If you want to pay using the credit card you have just entered, you can simply choose that option and your card will be automatically charged on a monthly basis as fees accrue.

If you would prefer to pay using a monthly direct debit you can select this option. The bank account you provided eBay with will be debited monthly if you complete the online direct debit mandate.

Fact: There is no subscription fee to sell on eBay. The only fees you pay are the ones you accrue when selling.

If you have used a debit card to register as a seller, the situation is slightly more complicated. eBay doesn't accept payment using debit cards. If you have used a Switch or Solo card you will have to set up a direct debit. If you do want to pay eBay using Switch or Solo you can make one-off payments via PayPal.

If you have any difficulties registering you have two options. First of all, try again and ensure that you have filled in all the details correctly. If you are still having difficulties you are best advised to contact eBay's Customer Support team who will be able to help you.

9

Prepare Your Listing

There are five key elements to a listing and you should have them all prepared before you even log on to eBay's Sell Your Item form:

- Category
- Item title and description
- Pictures
- Pricing
- Payment and postage details

When you list on eBay you enter your details into the online Sell Your Item form. Basically you will have to enter all the relevant information you want in your listing so eBay can build the page for you. If you have prepared all the information you need in advance, you will be able to fill in the Sell Your Item form quickly and easily.

Inside Information:
The Level Playing Field

You can compete with big corporations on eBay because it is a level playing field. This means that whether you are a hobby seller listing one item a month or a multinational corporation shifting thousands of units a week, you are treated just the same.

This is important because it preserves the vibrancy of the marketplace, making it a great place for people to buy and sell. If eBay became dominated by a small group of large retailers it would lose a lot of its charm. So if Big plc lists the same item as Mr Small Trader, they both pay the same fees and are subject to the same rules. And because they compete on a level playing field, their style of selling and how they treat customers count.

In many ways a small seller is more attractive to buyers because they know they can expect a more personal service and most likely a caring human to deal with. Small-scale traders can also be more flexible and nimble than outfits with dozens of employees. Smaller sellers can often provide greater satisfaction to their buyers and possibly be even more successful. On eBay, small can be beautiful and the real-world factors that favour established companies are swept away.

Choose a Category

As you will remember from your experiences as a buyer, the items for sale on eBay are organised under relevant headings in a category structure rather like in a library. So if you were looking on eBay for a first-edition copy of *The Old Devils* by Kingsley Amis, for instance, you would have gone to the Books category, clicked on First Editions and browsed under Fiction.

There are thousands of categories on eBay.co.uk and this is a mixed blessing. On the one hand it means you are certain to find one that is just right for the item you want to sell, but on the other it might take you a few moments to find it.

Choosing the right category is very important because it will help buyers locate your item. If your item is not in the best category, buyers won't be able to find it and you might lose out on a sale.

There are two ways to find the best category for the item you want to sell. The first is to browse the full list of categories. You can do this by clicking on 'Browse' in the Navigation Bar and pretending you are a buyer looking for your item.

The second option is to search for an item similar to the one you want to sell and see where other sellers are listing. You can do this using eBay's search engine by clicking on 'Search' in the Navigation Bar.

For many items you list, the choice of a category will be very straightforward. If you are listing a Minidisc player the obvious place will be in Consumer Electronics > Audio – Separates & Systems > MiniDisc.

If you are selling a Crocus-design Clarice Cliff plate, the most obvious and appropriate category is Pottery & Glass > Pottery > Clarice Cliff.

For other items you will need to think about who you consider will be most likely to buy the item when deciding which category to choose.

For example, if you have a framed and mounted stamp set featuring the late Queen Mother, an obvious category choice would be Stamps > UK (Great Britain) > Commemorative. But by choosing this category you will be pitching your item at stamp collectors. Would such an item be more likely to appeal to royal collectors in general? If so, you might be better off choosing Collectables > Royal Commemoratives > Queen Mother.

Imagine you have a *Lock, Stock and Two Smoking Barrels* poster signed by Vinnie Jones. You could list it in Collectables > Autographs > Film & TV. Perhaps DVD, Film & TV > Memorabilia: Posters > Originals – UK Quads would be better? Or if you think the football collectors might be more keen on it should you go for Sports > Football Memorabilia > Autographs? The decision is yours, depending on what you are selling.

Listing in Two Categories

You have the option to list your item in two categories if you like. But if you choose to do this, don't forget that your listing fees will be doubled (but not the Final Value Fees). Despite the extra costs, listing in two categories can be well worth it if you have an item of particular value or something that will be attractive to buyers in more than one field. Listing an item in two categories can greatly increase the chance of a sale.

Create an Item Title

Your Item Title and Description are where you get the opportunity to show off the item you are selling and persuade buyers that it is something they want to buy.

The Item Title is the name of the item you are selling and what buyers see first when they are searching or browsing. You need to ensure that your Item Title is as descriptive and eye-catching as possible so that buyers will be interested enough to look more closely at your item. You only have limited space for your Item Title and to make effective use of the space you will need to be inventive and precise.

If you were selling a Harry Potter book, you could just have a title that read 'Harry Potter Book'. But that wouldn't stand out from the thousands of other Harry Potter books for sale. In order to give yourself an edge, you need to think about what makes your item special and then distil the most important details into the short space. Which Harry Potter book is it? Which edition? Is it a hardback or a paperback? What kind of condition is the book in?

If you had a rare, first-edition, signed copy of *Harry Potter and the Chamber of Secrets* in mint condition, the Item Title could read 'Harry Potter Chamber of Secrets 1st Ed Signed'.

Whatever you are selling, the Item Title should consist of words a buyer is likely to search for. Avoid meaningless or vague terms ('old', 'good', 'nice', 'interesting' are not words people normally use when searching eBay). Stick to factual words that describe the item precisely, such as the brand, its size or type. If it is of an era or style such as Georgian or Art Deco or Retro, include this word as many people will use it to search.

The title is what eBay's search engine will use to make your item available to buyers, so think about how you search for items on eBay and employ that experience to make your item as findable as possible. If a buyer is interested in your Item Title, they will click on it to find out more.

Write a Description

Even if you are including photos in your listing, it is vital to compose an Item Description that tells buyers as much about the item as possible. Give as many details as you can about the item and its condition. Again, put yourself in a buyer's shoes and imagine what you would want to know if you were considering placing a bid.

Talk the item up. Leave the buyer in no doubt that this is the item they want and give them reasons to place a bid. Be creative and don't be afraid to be personal. If the item is unusual or rare, explain how you got hold of it. Go into as much detail as you can. People like eBay because they are buying from other individuals and not giant, faceless corporations. Show that you are caring, individual and concerned. Taking the time to compile your description is an important way of building trust.

It is essential to be full and honest. Don't just include all the plus points; if there is damage or something that affects the quality of the item, mention that too. Failure to disclose something now could result in negative Feedback later.

Imagine you have a rare Doctor Who video for sale. A hastily assembled description would read: 'Dr Who Video "Shada". Rare, in almost perfect condition.'

This Item Description would suffice, but a few extra moments honing the description could reap bigger rewards: 'Dr Who video "Shada" BBCV 4814. This classic Tom Baker adventure, also starring Lalla Ward as Romana II, was written by Douglas Adams and is set in Cambridge. Never originally completed for broadcast in 1978 due to BBC strikes, the fragments that do exist have been linked by superb and often bizarre commentary from Baker. This adventure is now considered a classic by Who fans and the 1992 video is highly sought after. The item is in almost perfect condition with a small scuff on the spine of the video and comes complete with the script book as originally released. The video is in the PAL format and is not compatible with American (NTSC) video machines. An absolute must to complete any Whovian's video collection.'

Although you have the option to give further details later, it is wise to include some information in the Item Description about payment and postage. Explain briefly what payment methods you are willing to take and what the postage costs will be.

• **Returns and refunds** It isn't obligatory to have a policy on refunds and returns. Some buyers like the peace of mind of buying from a seller who will refund if the buyer is not satisfied with the item when they receive it. It's a good way of building trust and as long as you are honest in your description you will probably never need to use it. Take a look around the site for examples of what other sellers offer.

• **Preparation** Write your Title and Description in Microsoft Word (or any wordprocessing software) in advance. This means that when it comes to logging on to the Sell Your Item form you can just copy and paste what you have already written into the right boxes.

• **Know your item** If you don't know much about your item, eBay itself is a good source of information. Search the site for items like yours. Don't forget that there are countless collector and expert websites that can also be a good source of information. Use a search engine such as Google to find out more about the item you are selling.

• **Specialist terms** Be careful about misusing specialist terms. Books, records and stamps in particular have a whole host of specialist terms that dealers use to describe items. If you misuse a term and misdescribe the item you will have an irate buyer on your hands.

• **Keep it basic** Some sellers like to customise their Item Description so it is bright and colourful. Some even include animation and fancy effects. Not only do effects irritate some buyers, they can also take a long time to load if the buyer has a slow connection. It is best to keep your description clear and basic so it is easy for buyers to understand. Don't forget that you don't need to use HTML; eBay will do all the formatting for you on the Sell Your Item form.

Tip

Many sellers organise their Item Descriptions by using bullet points because buyers find this an easy way to absorb a lot of information quickly.

Creating Good Photographs

Including pictures in your listing is vital. If you want to get the best possible price you have to encourage bidders that yours is the item they want and that you are a seller they can trust. One way of really putting a buyer's mind at rest and assuring them that they want your item is to provide a picture.

Inside Information:
Bad Pictures and Hilarious Mistakes

Bad pictures can be found all over eBay. Considering how easy it is to create a useful picture and how important a good picture is to buyers, it's astonishing how many really awful pictures you see. I can't claim to be Lord Lichfield, but I always take the time to create a picture that will clinch the deal when I have an item for sale.

Why don't other sellers do the same? I honestly don't know. Maybe they are too busy listing dozens of items. Maybe they just don't understand the power of a good photo. What I do know is that a minute spent creating the perfect image can reap the rewards of more bids and a better price.

When you are taking your picture, however, be careful that you aren't giving away too much: remember the very famous example of the man and the kettle. It was a handsome kettle made of metal and burnished to a gleaming sheen; so shiny was it that in the picture the seller was reflected in the surface of the kettle as if it were a mirror. This would only have been a minor distraction, of course, had the photographer been wearing any clothes when snapping his item ready for sale on eBay. If he hadn't been naked the picture wouldn't have been passed around the internet and seen by millions of people. It's a cautionary tale: make sure you check your pictures for unintentional details.

Needless to say, some people have seen the humorous accidental picture phenomenon and taken it to its illogical conclusion. When someone takes a picture that deliberately includes a reflection of themselves in the nude it's called Reflectoporn. It's difficult to know whether to laugh or cry. I

*imagine that some people do it for the thrill; others have no
idea that their mistake is amusing hundreds of thousands of
people. But you do see it sometimes, so keep an eye out.*

Why Photos Are Important

Remember that buyers on eBay don't get the opportunity to
handle or examine the item until they receive it in the post, so by
providing a picture you are giving them the opportunity to see the
item online before they bid. eBay sellers are agreed: pictures
encourage buyers to bid with more confidence. If you don't have
a picture in your listing you are limiting your chances of a successful sale.

There are a number of ways you can capture a digital image
to use in your listing. You could use a digital camera or scanner
and nowadays you can get hold of one relatively cheaply. Many
computer packages come complete with a scanner. If you don't
have a digital camera or scanner, try to borrow one if you can
because a picture will enhance your listing dramatically. If you
only have a conventional film camera you could use that. Many
film-developing companies offer a service that means you can get
your prints as usual but also receive a set of digital images on CD,
which you can then use on eBay.

With such an enormous selection of cameras and scanners on
the market it would be impossible here to provide precise guid-
ance on how to produce images with your particular apparatus.

For the purposes of selling on eBay all you need is an image
saved on to your computer and ready to upload to the website.
For detailed instructions on how to capture images using your
digital camera or scanner, you should consult the manufacturer's
manual. To use eBay's Picture Service to host your images you
will need to save the image in a jpeg (.jpg) format.

More about Photographs

Simply including a picture isn't enough. Your picture needs to
provide the buyer with information that will be useful.

• **Show your item off** Ensure that the image you produce is
sharp and in focus; blurred photos don't impress. Consider
what the buyer wants to see. If you are selling a book, for
instance, is the front cover what a buyer wants to see or is a

shot of the inside of the book more useful? Will a buyer appreciate a close-up image of the markings or serial number? Record collectors often value a close-up of the label on the record itself rather than merely the sleeve. If you are selling an item in its original box, then removing the item is usually best (unless of course it means that the item is worthless because it has been opened), rather than offering a view of a cardboard box.

Photograph your item from the most useful aspect, remembering that the obvious picture may not be the most useful. Good lighting can also make a world of difference.

• **Compose a useful image** The setting and background of the image are also important. Avoid photographing your item in a way that distracts from the item or causes confusion. Photograph your item against a blank background, perhaps by using a sheet or cloth. Make sure your item is the central feature of the picture.

• **Consider using several pictures** If your item is of high value or there are different aspects you want to show, don't forget that you can use more than one image in your listing. You can include a number of pictures so you can show different angles and details as you wish.

• **Digital cameras** You don't need a top-of-the-range digital camera to produce the pictures you need for your listing. Perfectly adequate images can be created with a one or two mega (million) pixel camera. Even a clear, well-composed image taken using the camera in your mobile phone could do the trick.

Decide Your Pricing

Setting the price you want for an item is a delicate balancing act. Obviously you will have a price in mind, but equally you don't want to price yourself out of the market.

• **Check the price of similar items** You can get a feel for the price that items similar to yours fetch by checking on eBay. You can either search or browse as you would as a buyer to find similar items and keep an eye on them to see how they go. Another option is to do a search for Completed Items. This will show you the items that have recently ended and you will be able to check the price they sold for.

To search for Completed Items, click 'Advanced Search' in the Navigation Bar. You can then Search Completed Items in the usual way with keywords and the Completed Items option.

• **Set a realistic price** eBay is a very competitive marketplace. There are other sellers out there who may well have a similar item for sale. If a buyer can get the same item cheaper elsewhere, they will. You should set a starting price that is the lowest amount you are willing to let your item go for. Be realistic about the price you set and remember that buyers will often bid up an item if they want it badly.

Inside Information: Pricing

Why not price your item a little bit lower than the comparable items on the site? You will get more attention and probably more bids. Think about it. If you have included all the right keywords in your Item Title and your listing is returned alongside identical ones, the price will often be the deciding factor when it comes to making a bid. I've found that if I start my items at a slightly lower price than the competition then in the end I get a better price than them: buyers get carried away and bid more because they are determined to beat other bidders.

Some sellers like to take a gamble and start their items at 99p even if the item is worth much more. This is because they have confidence in the eBay system and are sure that the item will find its true eBay value. The low start price means lower eBay listing fees, but there is a risk. If the bidding doesn't get going, you will have to let the item go for 99p if you only get one bid.

Always think about eBay's fees when you list an item. For instance, if you want to list your item with a starting price of £5 you should list it for £4.99 because the eBay Listing Fee

*will be 20p rather than 30p. Familiarise yourself with eBay's
fees so you can minimise the price you pay to list your item.*

Setting a Reserve Price

eBay offers the option to set a Reserve Price on auctions, but you
should think carefully whether one will be useful. A Reserve
Price on eBay is a bit different to those found in an auction
house. If you use a reserve on eBay, you can set the bidding
going at a low price but you are not obliged to let the item go
unless it reaches the reserve you have set. The reserve isn't
revealed to the bidders. For instance, if you have an item you
think is worth £60 you can set a Starting Price of 1p (which will
excite bidders chasing a bargain), but you won't sell the item
until someone bids £60 or more. Any Reserve Price you set must
be above £50, so it isn't available if you are selling lower-value
items.

Some buyers say they are put off by Reserve Prices. There
are also extra selling costs for setting a Reserve Price since, even
if you start the item off at a penny, eBay's listing fee will be
based on the Reserve you set. There is also an additional fee for
using a Reserve Price. This is refunded if the item sells.

Generally, setting a reserve complicates a sale, so until you
are a confident seller it is advisable not to use them.

Decide Your Payment and Postage Details

Including information about how buyers can pay you and how
much it will cost to send the buyer the item is vital.

• **Payment methods** Often when people are new to eBay
selling the first question they ask is: 'How do I receive the
money?' The simple answer is: 'It's up to you.' On eBay you
are free to determine the terms under which you sell your
item and when it comes to payment options you can choose
to receive payment in whatever form is convenient for you.
Cheques and postal orders are easy to accept but you can also
opt for online services such as PayPal. For bulky items that
need collection or if a buyer is close by and wants to come
and collect the item, you can accept cash on collection.

• **PayPal for sellers** As you will have discovered when you were buying on eBay, PayPal is an attractive way of sending payment because it is quick and easy. It is very handy for buyers because there is no cost and they don't have to write a cheque, buy a stamp and go to the postbox. As a seller you do incur a charge for accepting PayPal, but many sellers agree that the cost is worth it. Many take the PayPal fees into account when they list their item and incorporate it into the starting price or postage costs. Cashing cheques means a trip to the bank and waiting for clearance, which can take days. An immediate payment via PayPal means you can despatch the item immediately and turn around your sales much more quickly.

PayPal is also a very useful way of accepting payment from overseas. When you are selling on eBay it is worth thinking about whether you are happy to send your item abroad rather than restricting it only to British buyers. The obvious advantage of offering your item to overseas buyers is that there are many more potential buyers. eBay was founded in the USA and has millions of members there; and don't forget its growing communities in Europe and Asia. With PayPal your buyer can pay in their own currency using their credit or debit card and PayPal will take care of the currency conversion.

There are several other online payment methods that you can accept. None is as widely used as PayPal or offers the flexibility of international trading in the same way.

On the Sell Your Item form you can note the payment methods you are willing to accept. Offer as many as you can. The more options you provide, the more flexibility you are offering your buyers.

• **Postage costs** When you are selling on eBay it is essential to state the postage costs of your item up front. For many buyers the postage costs are the deciding factor: if your postage charges are too high you will put people off.

The more details you can provide for international buyers the better, but at the very least you should state the cost of posting the item within the UK.

Postage and Packaging Tips

To attract buyers you should keep your postal charges as low as possible. After all, if it is a toss-up between your item and a similar item from another seller, the cost of postage can be the deciding factor.

- **Keep postage costs low** Postage and packaging costs should be exactly that: the costs of protecting the item in transit and the price of the postage. eBay does allow sellers some leeway and lets you add some additional handling costs, although they shouldn't be excessive. High charges put buyers off.

- **Scales and rates** Within the UK, the Royal Mail and Parcelforce are usually the most convenient and cost-effective carriers. It is well worth familiarising yourself with the published rates at www.royalmail.com. Additionally, as most eBayers will know, your local post office will be able to advise. Get to know the people there. If you are successful on eBay you will almost certainly be a frequent visitor.

Your other best friend will be your kitchen scales. Once you are armed with the Royal Mail rates you can weigh the items and make a good estimate of the postage costs. Buyers always like to know the price of postage and by giving accurate quotes you will seem like a professional and organised seller. The scales will also ensure that you do not underquote and lose money.

- **International shipping** For items up to 2kg (5kg for printed matter) that need to go overseas, the Royal Mail is also the most convenient carrier. On international shipments you can save your buyers money by making use of the different options available. Surface mail takes longer than air mail, but it is also much cheaper and many buyers will be willing to wait if it means they can save money. Also, where appropriate, ensure that your items are sent using the small packet rate because this is cheaper than the letter rate. If you are selling books, comics or magazines you can make use of the preferential rates offered for printed matter.

• **Packaging** Don't forget to factor the packaging costs into your postage charges. It is vital to ensure that the item you send is packaged well and totally protected.

It pays to be inventive with packaging. Buyers don't necessarily want expensive packaging and will be happy to receive a parcel that looks amateurish with an intact purchase inside rather than a very smart package that hasn't protected the item at all.

Many sellers recycle old padded envelopes or boxes. Very strong 'envelopes' can be fashioned from cardboard boxes and brown tape. Consider reusing bubble wrap, packing peanuts or other items you receive your purchases in. As long as the savings you are making are reflected in what the buyer pays, you won't receive any complaints. However, if you charge for new packaging and then recycle, you might have an irate buyer to deal with because they will know you are pocketing the difference.

Listing Enhancements

When you are selling an item you will want it to stand out from the many others for sale. A Listing Enhancement is a way to pay for your item to have a greater profile when a buyer is browsing or searching eBay. There are different enhancements available depending on the prominence you want to give the item and what you are willing to spend. The fees for Listing Enhancements are payable regardless of whether your item sells or not.

• **Gallery** Adding your item to the Gallery is probably the best use of your money if you want to buy a Listing Enhancement. For only 15p a Gallery listing allows a member who is searching or browsing to see the picture of your item you have added in the Listings themselves.

• **Bold** You can make your Item Title appear in bold in the Listings for 75p.

• **Highlight** If you want your item to stand out a bit more you can have it highlighted in a purple-coloured band for £1.50.

• **Featured Gallery** For £15.95 not only will your item appear in the Gallery but it will appear at the top of the Gallery list when other members are browsing or searching. This is an expensive feature and you should ensure it will work for you before investing the money.

• **Featured Plus** If you opt for Featured Plus your item will be in the Featured Items section at the top of Listings pages. Featured Plus costs £9.95 and if you combine it with a Gallery enhancement it will give you more prominence than the more expensive Featured Gallery enhancement.

• **HomePage Featured** Unless you are selling something very expensive or special, you shouldn't need to use Homepage Featured. It costs £49.95, gives your item the most prominence in Featured Items sections across the site and means that your item may also appear on the eBay.co.uk homepage.

Inside Information:
The Gallery Is Great

If you really want to get a big bang for your buck, choose the Gallery. Adding your item to the Gallery costs 15p on top of your basic listing fee and, depending on what you are selling and for how much, adding your item to the Gallery can be well worth the money.

When buyers are browsing or searching eBay they are often presented with lists of Item Titles. I don't need to tell you that sometimes these lists can seem rather dull. A Gallery picture really can make your item stand out.

For items that are very striking and well photographed, the added profile the Gallery provides can be great value for money. Also, if your item has a high value the added attention can really pay off.

10 Listing Your Item

Preparing your listing before you even log on to eBay is the key to selling your item successfully. Only when you have sorted out a picture and a description and decided all the other important things for your listing are you ready to list your item on eBay.

Inside Information:
Timing Your Sales

There are no hard-and-fast rules on what will work best for your sales. The orthodox view is that ending your listings on a Sunday evening is the best plan: lots of sellers start their listing on a Thursday evening so they get two weekends and end on a Sunday evening. But recently sellers I have spoken to seem to think that avoiding Sunday evening altogether is advisable, because so many items end then.

It's easier to advise on what you should avoid. Try not to have your items ending on a Friday morning between 9am and 11am because this is when eBay tends to do its scheduled maintenance to the site. Although the site is generally operational, some sections of it are not available.

Also avoid clashes with major events, especially if they are related to the item you are selling. The last hour of your listing is when much of the bidding will take place, so make sure it's going to suit bidders. It would be a bit silly to end a listing for a Big Brother-*related item while the eviction is on the television. Equally, if everyone in the nation is glued to their screens watching a big game, your England football shirt might not get the bids it deserves.*

Don't forget international bidders. If your item is likely to be attractive to buyers in America, you can adjust the timing so it finishes later in the evening in the UK but in the early evening on the other side of the Atlantic.

As you sell more you start to learn what works for you, so you can experiment with timings. For instance, I have noticed on my own sales that workday lunchtimes, especially on Monday, seem to be a good time. I reckon there are thousands of bored office workers chomping on their sandwiches and bidding on eBay to alleviate the post-weekend blues and hoping for a bargain.

The Sell Your Item Form

To list your item on eBay and make it available for people to buy, you need to put everything you have prepared into the Sell Your Item form. This is a series of online pages that allows you to build the View Item page that buyers see.

It isn't a difficult process, but it can be a little daunting for beginners because you are required to answer questions and provide details that you might not have thought of. But don't be nervous: lots of people list items on eBay and if it they can do it, so can you.

And don't forget, if you do get it wrong you can always go back and edit your listing or even scrap it and start again.

• **Just take your time** When you are an experienced seller listing an item will only take a few moments, probably less than five minutes. But new sellers often say that their first listing took half an hour or maybe longer. So don't worry if you feel like you're making little progress or going very slowly; everyone was slow the first time. As you become familiar with the process it gets quicker and easier, so don't be afraid to take a bit of time and really get a feel for how you list an item. Have a relaxing cup of tea or a glass of beer by your side to keep you going.

• **How do I find the Sell Your Item form?** You can get to the Sell Your Item form by clicking on 'Sell' in the Navigation Bar. You'll need to sign in using your User ID and password.

Choose a Selling Format

On the first page of the Sell Your Item form you choose the selling format for your listing. This means you need to choose between the traditional auction format, where buyers bid for your item, and the Buy It Now option, where people don't bid but simply buy your item at a price specified by you.

For your first sale, choose the auction format. This way you'll get a real feel for how eBay works. You can experiment with Buy It Now when you have found your eBay feet. In fact, if this is your first sale you probably won't be able to choose Buy It Now. To use it you need to have 10 or more Feedbacks or have given eBay your direct debit details. If you don't qualify to use Buy It Now you can just click the 'Continue' button at the bottom of the page. If you can use it, select 'Sell at Online Auction' and then click 'Continue'.

Select a Category

You'll already know which category you want your item to be listed in if you've prepared and found out where other sellers list similar items. If you already know, this stage will only take a moment. All you need to do is select the top-level category, such as 'Stamps' or 'Toys & Games', in the first box on the lefthand side.

Once you have made your selection another list will show you the next level of categories. Keep on choosing and moving from box to box until there are no more options to take. It'll require three or four clicks. Once you have made your choice, simply click 'Continue' to go to the next page.

If you haven't already decided which category you want to list your item in, eBay can help you. You can enter keywords related to your item such as 'Prada purse' or 'Belgian Army

Sell Your Item: Select Category

| 1 Category | 2. Title & Description | 3. Pictures & Details | 4. Payment & Postage | 5. Review & Submit |

Main Category * Required

Click below to choose a previously used category, or click in the boxes to select a new category. When finished, click **Continue.**

Enter item keywords to find a category

[   ] Find Tips

For example, "gold bracelet" not "jewelery"

Browse categories

Click a category in each box until the last box turns gray

Antiques & Art -->
Automotive -->
Books, Comics & Magazines -->
Business, Office & Industrial -->
Clothes, Shoes & Accessories -->
Coins -->
Collectables -->
Computing -->
Consumer Electronics -->

Clear selection

Having difficulty viewing the category selector? Try this one.

Second category

List your item in a second category! (Fee varies)
Listing in two categories has been shown to increase final price on average by 18%.

< Back   Continue >

helmet' and eBay will make some suggestions. This might be handy, but it doesn't beat taking the time to choose the category that is absolutely right for your item.

If the category selector isn't visible on the screen this might be because your PC can't view certain types of computer code. You have the option to use the same function in a different format by clicking the link under the category selector.

You can opt to list your item in two categories rather than just one by clicking the 'List your item in a second category' link. This might be a good way to attract more buyers, but don't forget it will double all your listing fees, so only choose this option if you think it's worth it.

Describe Your Item

Describing your item will be a doddle because you will have already written your Title and Item Description and have it ready to paste into this page. Simply copy the title from a Word document and paste it into the title space. You can do the same with your description. Just copy and paste the description you prepared earlier into the appropriate space.

Like in most wordprocessing programs, you can change the look of your text by highlighting sections or the whole document and change the font, size and colour. You can also alter the alignment of the text and emphasise key details by making them bold, italic or underlined.

If you are a computer whizz and have prepared your description using HTML, you need to switch to the 'Enter your own HTML' tab. If you enter HTML into the normal description field it won't work.

If you want to see how your description will look when it's live on the site to make sure it's how you want it, click the 'Preview Description' link near the bottom of the page.

Tip

If there are key details about your item that you think will grab someone's attention and make them bid, you can add a 'Subtitle' to your item. This is an additional short description under the Item Title that will be visible in Search and Browse. Adding a Subtitle costs an additional 50p, so you should only use it if you think it's worth it and have already run out of space in your title.

Enter Pictures and Item Details

This is the longest page of the Sell Your Item form and on your first sale you'll need to enter some important information. When you list again the Sell Your Item form will remember some of this, so it won't take as long to fill in this section a second time. Some of the information you need to enter on this page is compulsory. If you need to make a selection the field is marked with a green star. You cannot progress to the next page until you have entered all the required information.

- **Price** First of all you need to select your Starting Price. This is the minimum price you are willing to sell your item for. From your general knowledge and research into similar items on eBay, you will know what your item might sell for. You enter the Starting Price in the first field.

- **Duration** You are also required to select how long you want your listing to last for. You have a choice of 1, 3, 5, 7 or 10 days: how long your listing lasts for has no bearing on fees. You should choose whatever suits you best: 7 or 10 days are the most popular options, but if you are selling concert tickets or something else that is time sensitive a shorter duration might suit you better.

- **Quantity and location** In the 'Quantity' field you should note how many different items you have for sale. Typically this will be just one, but sometimes you might have a Lot or Multiple Items.

You must also state where you and the item are. You can be boring and just say 'London' or 'Middlesbrough', depending where you are. But it can be worth being more specific, like 'Putney, London SW15'. Or you can interest buyers by including something more romantic and attractive like 'The Wild North East of England'. It's up to you.

• **Pictures** If you haven't got a picture ready by the time you reach this stage of the Sell Your Item form, it's a bit late to get your digital camera out and take one. If you have one prepared all you need to do is upload it to eBay.

The first time you upload a picture you'll need to install a small bit of software from eBay on your computer. This won't take a minute and you won't need to do it again. eBay will guide you through the download step by step.

eBay offers all sorts of advanced picture options that can be useful. Its pictures appear in a standard format of 400×300 pixels, which is roughly the size of a cigarette packet on screen. For most items this is more than enough, but sometimes you might want to show your items in greater detail. For 60p you can supersize your pictures so they appear larger. The Slide Show option is also 60p. This displays several images of what you are selling in succession so buyers really get a feel for the item. The Picture Pack options mean you can supersize your images, use the Slide Show and have up to six images all for 90p. For £1.35 you can have the same but use between seven and twelve images. What you choose depends on what you are selling and how you need to show it off, but for a big-ticket item investing a few extra pence can be well worth it.

If you like you have the option to host your photographs on your own webspace. Hosting your own images can take a bit longer than letting eBay do it, but it can be worthwhile. eBay will host one image for free, so if you want more than one you can either pay for them or keep them on your own website. eBay automatically crops and edits your pictures, but if you do your own they can be as big or as small as you like. Nevertheless, for a first-time seller eBay's picture service is more than adequate and by far the easiest option.

If you want to add your picture to the Gallery you need to tick the box at the bottom of the 'Add Pictures' section.

• **Counters** Including a Counter is free, so there's no reason not to have one. A counter shows you how many people have taken a look at your View Item page. This can be a great way of gauging interest and letting you know whether you are attracting people to your listing.

Tip

This page is the most confusing in the Sell Your Item form because there are so many things you can choose from. If something isn't marked with a green star you don't have to express a preference.

The options highlighted so far are the most important. Some are compulsory while others are free and useful. Sometimes you might want to make use of the extras on offer on the Sell Your Item form. Most of them have an additional charge attached, but for the right item and seller they can mean better sales.

- **Schedule your listing** If you want your item to start, and therefore end, at a particular time but can't be at your computer then, you can choose to schedule your listing. This means you can create the listing and send it to eBay immediately, but it won't be available to buyers on the site until a time you specify. The option to schedule a listing costs 12p and you can do so up to three weeks in advance.

- **Listing designer** If you want to give your item a really professional and jazzy look, you can choose a Listing Designer template from the selection eBay has available. This is a graphical border that will set your Item Description off to a tee. Depending on what you are selling you can choose a theme or colour scheme that will complement it. Adding a Listing Designer template will cost you an additional 7p, so it can be well worth it if you are selling a high-priced item. Sci-fi fans should check out the 'Space Cow' theme.

- **Listing enhancements** If you want to utilise one of these you need to do it on this section of the Sell Your Item Form.

- **Private auction** Sometimes people like some anonymity. If you hold a Private Auction no one can see the identities of the bidders. This can be particularly useful if you are selling something very, very unusual (which people might want to be secretive about owning) or something people might be embarrassed to be seen buying. Otherwise, don't use this option. It is free, but it can put off buyers who don't understand the reason for keeping identities hush-hush and are scared away by the cloak-and-dagger approach.

Enter Payment and Postage

You're in the home straight by the time you have to specify your Payment and Postage preferences.

You should accept PayPal as an absolute minimum and any other payment options that suit you. The Sell Your Item form automatically assumes that your PayPal-registered email address is the same as the one you have given to eBay. If it isn't, you should add your PayPal email address here. eBay will remember it for when you list in future.

You can also indicate here whether you are willing to accept other payment methods such as a cheque, Postal Order or escrow.

If you are willing to accept a cheque or other payment that will be sent in the post, eBay will assume that you want it to be sent to your registered address. If you want it to be sent to a different address you'll need to enter it by clicking the 'Change' link under the 'Seller's Payment Address' heading.

It is best to provide a postage cost for UK-based buyers in the field provided because it will save you time later. This can be easily calculated and means that a British buyer can make a PayPal payment immediately at the end of the listing if they wish. You can also indicate international postage costs if you like.

- **Payment instructions and returns policy** Even though you have specified how much UK postage will be and the payment methods you are willing to accept, it is probable you will need to include some extra details to assist your buyers. For instance, you might want to note that you expect payment within 14 days, that you prefer PayPal or that international bidders should contact you for further details about overseas postage costs.

If you are willing to accept returns or offer refunds, this space in the Sell Your Item form is the ideal place to provide your terms.

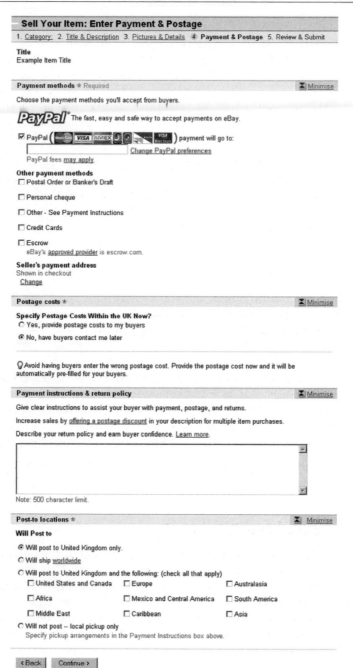

Sell Your Item: Enter Payment & Postage

1. Category: 2. Title & Description   3. Pictures & Details   ④ Payment & Postage   5. Review & Submit

Title
Example Item Title

Payment methods ∗ Required   ✕ Minimise

Choose the payment methods you'll accept from buyers.

PayPal The fast, easy and safe way to accept payments on eBay.

☑ PayPal (VISA AMEX VISA Electron) payment will go to:

[   ]   Change PayPal preferences
PayPal fees may apply.

Other payment methods
☐ Postal Order or Banker's Draft

☐ Personal cheque

☐ Other - See Payment Instructions

☐ Credit Cards

☐ Escrow
eBay's approved provider is escrow.com.

Seller's payment address
Shown in checkout
Change

Postage costs ∗   ✕ Minimise

Specify Postage Costs Within the UK Now?
○ Yes, provide postage costs to my buyers
◉ No, have buyers contact me later

💡 Avoid having buyers enter the wrong postage cost. Provide the postage cost now and it will be automatically pre-filled for your buyers.

Payment instructions & return policy   ✕ Minimise

Give clear instructions to assist your buyer with payment, postage, and returns.

Increase sales by offering a postage discount in your description for multiple item purchases.

Describe your return policy and earn buyer confidence. Learn more.

```



```

Note: 500 character limit.

Post-to locations ∗   ✕ Minimise

Will Post to

◉ Will post to United Kingdom only.

○ Will ship worldwide

○ Will post to United Kingdom and the following: (check all that apply)
     ☐ United States and Canada   ☐ Europe   ☐ Australasia

     ☐ Africa   ☐ Mexico and Central America   ☐ South America

     ☐ Middle East   ☐ Caribbean   ☐ Asia

○ Will not post -- local pickup only
     Specify pickup arrangements in the Payment Instructions box above.

[‹ Back]   [Continue ›]

Tip

Much of the information you enter on the Sell Your Item form is common to all your listings. You only need to enter it once and eBay will remember it. Once the information is stored you can make the form easier to navigate by clicking the 'Minimise' buttons on the righthand side of the page. When you do this you won't see the options and your stored details will be used until you change them.

• **Post-to locations** Where you are willing to send your item to is up to you, but you should be aware that it also determines who can see your item and the number of potential buyers who can bid. By choosing 'Will Post Worldwide' your item will be available to all eBay members all over the world. If your item is only going to be attractive to UK buyers, or is too bulky to send overseas, then the 'Will Post to the United Kingdom Only' option will be best for you.

You can pick and choose your options here. If you want to ship to the United States and Canada as well as the UK, or just the UK and Asia, it's totally up to you.

Tip

By entering these details now you are making it easy for your buyer to pay at the end of the auction. When your listing ends successfully your buyer will automatically receive an email from eBay with all the instructions they need to make their payment. If you don't enter them now you'll have to email the buyer yourself at the end of the auction.

Review and Submit Listing

Once you get to this point you're pretty much ready to send your item live to site and make it available to buyers. This is your opportunity to ensure that the listing you have created is ship-shape and Bristol fashion.

All the information you have submitted is available for your review and you have the opportunity to go back and edit it as you wish by choosing the appropriate link on the lefthand side of the page.

Take a moment to examine the listing fees that eBay will be charging you. They will be detailed at the bottom of the page and won't be charged until you submit the listing. If you have chosen a feature you don't want to pay for, you can go back and remove it from this page. If you want to add additional features you can go back and add them too.

When you're happy with your listing, all you need to do is click 'Submit Listing' at the bottom of the page and your item is complete. eBay starts to weave its magic and it will be added to the Search index and the category you chose.

Congratulations!

You've listed your first item on eBay! Now the excitement begins. Usually a listing is available to buyers within a few minutes of your completing it, but sometimes it can take a few hours for it to appear so don't panic if you can't find it immediately. You'll be able to access it from 'My eBay' or if you want you can search or browse for it like a buyer would.

If you go searching for your listing and you notice that it isn't exactly as you want it, you can even edit it when it is live. You can find out how to revise and add to your listing in the next chapter.

Other Sell Your Item Options

Depending on what you are selling, there are two other features you might see on the Sell Your Item form when you are listing your item: Item Specifics and Pre-Filled Item Information. Both are useful and free.

Item Specifics

When you were learning about eBay as a buyer, you will have come across the 'Product Finder' on the lefthand side of search and browse listings. For instance, if you searched for 'Paul Simon' in the Music sections, you had the opportunity to narrow down your search by choosing just to look at the CDs found in the results or those that were unplayed and 'Never Opened'.

The Product Finder is not available in every category, but where it exists it is an easy way of locating the item you want to buy. As a seller you should take advantage of it and make sure your item is available to buyers who like to use it.

It only takes a few moments on the Sell Your Item form to add the 'Item Specifics' that the Product Finder needs to locate your items. If this function is available in the category you are listing in, an 'Item Specifics' section will be visible in same section where you add your Item Title and Description.

All you need to do is select the values that best match your item. If you can't find one that matches, you don't need to choose one. In fact, if you don't want to choose Item Specifics at all you don't have to: it is totally optional.

For instance, if you were selling a CD of *Definitely Maybe* by Oasis that you had listened to a bit over the years, you would choose 'Indie/BritPop' as the genre, 'Album' as the format, and the condition as 'Played'.

The choices are slightly different if you choose to use Item Specifics in DVDs, Videos or Automotive or whatever, but the principle is the same.

Pre-filled Item Information

Pre-filled Item Information is available if you are selling CDs, DVDs or cars. eBay takes a lot of the grubby work out of listing an item by providing you with catalogue information to include in your listing. For instance, if you are selling a DVD and you enter the EAN number from the back of the box, your item will automatically include details of the film such as the cast, running time, a basic plot description and a stock photograph. For a CD you'll get the track listing and some notes and reviews.

Obviously this is going to save a bit of time, but it doesn't mean you don't have any work to do. The catalogue information that eBay provides for free is just the common information every single item of the same kind has. You will still need to include information that is only true for your particular item: good and bad. If your item comes complete with extras that others may lack, add those details. If your item has been damaged then you should note that too, just as you would if you were writing your own description from scratch.

Be different

Using Pre-filled Item Information isn't an excuse for being lazy. It will save you a slab of time, but if you really want your listing to work you need to be clever. For instance, because anyone can use Pre-Filled Item Information, the chances are that there will be items that look very similar. In particular you need to pay attention to the Item Title. This will be provided, but it will be identical to everyone else's. Add to, amend and improve the Item Title so your item stands out from the crowd.

11 / Managing Your Listing

Once your listing is live on eBay and available to buyers, you don't have the luxury of simply sitting back and relaxing until it ends. You still have a little work to do. Taking the time to manage your listing can win you more bids and a better price.

First things first: sit tight and try not to worry. Lots of first-time sellers worry when the item they are selling doesn't get any bids in the first few days of the auction. Commonly they worry that they have made an error or that buyers can't find the item. This is usually not case. On eBay, just like at real auctions, bidders like to keep their powder dry. Rushing in and placing a bid early on is considered by many buyers to be a surefire way of pushing up the final price.

The vast majority of bids on eBay are placed in the final 24 hours of a listing and often you will see the bulk of bidding going on in the closing minutes. This can make the first days of a listing seem dull for the seller who worries that no one is going to buy what they are selling. But just because people aren't bidding it doesn't mean that they aren't looking at your listing and deciding whether it is for them.

Inside Information:
Selling Surprises

Sometimes when you are selling an item you get a surprise. A good surprise. If you don't know much about the item you are selling, it could turn out to be worth much more than you imagine.

Two great eBay selling stories stand out as examples. The first is about a seller in America who discovered a beer bottle in his attic. It was old and dusty, but the seller knew there was a market for collectable breweriana so he chanced his luck and listed it on eBay, starting the bidding at a dollar.

Little did he know that the bottle he had was something of a Holy Grail among collectors. The bidding got off to a good start. Soon the word was out and he was astonished when the bids were in the hundreds of dollars. Collectors from all over America were emailing him asking for more details. When the auction ended the seller netted $19,000 for a bottle he might otherwise have thrown away.

A similar story involves a seller who put up a fishing lure or fly on eBay. He didn't know that the fly was a very rare example from a well-respected maker: it sold for $32,000.

Closer to home there are some fascinating examples of runaway bidding that have amazed sellers. On the UK Discussion Boards there's a member who bought a record at a car boot sale for 5p and sold it on eBay for more than £500. It isn't uncommon to read about sellers who pick up an item for a quid or two and sell it on for £20, £30, £40 or more.

The moral of these stories is twofold. It proves the old maxim that one person's junk is another person's treasure. The stuff you have gathering dust in your loft may well be the one-off collectables other people spend a lifetime seeking.

Secondly, it demonstrates that if you're going to sell something you don't know much about, eBay is the place. If the sellers of the beer bottle or the fishing fly had been at a car boot sale they might have raised a few dollars because they didn't know any better. A chuffed collector who couldn't believe their luck would have scuttled off with a very smug grin on their face and the bargain of their lives. On eBay buyers have to battle with each other and when there are lots of bidders who want to buy an item, the seller stands the best chance of getting the price they deserve.

My eBay

You can easily track your listings by using My eBay. To find the item you are selling, click on the 'All Selling' tab in My eBay and a list of the items you are selling will be there for you to examine, just as they are when you're buying items. My eBay summarises whether your item has bids, the current price and the time the listing ends. You can access My eBay by clicking on the 'My eBay' link at the top of most eBay pages and signing in using your User ID and Password.

If you want to take a closer look at the item you are selling, simply click on the Item Title in My eBay and you will be taken to the View Item page. From there you can examine your high bidder and see what the current price is. By clicking 'Bid History' you can see more details about the bidding activity and all the bids you have received. You can also check out the bidders themselves by examining their Feedback, as you would with a seller.

To reassure yourself that people really are able to find your listing and are taking the time to check it out, scroll down the View Item page and see how many visitors you've had. The counter you included in your listing will tell you how many people have looked at the item.

If people like the look of your item and think they might want to place a bid later in the auction, they will add your item to their Watch List. You can see how many watchers you have in My eBay.

Respond to Emails

However detailed and full your description is, buyers will often contact you directly with questions requiring further information or clarification. The emails will be forwarded to your registered email address by eBay. Your email address is not disclosed to people who ask you a question. Take the time to answer these questions honestly and quickly, because that gives a good impression and shows you are a good seller.

Sometimes you might get an email from a member asking you to end the auction early and sell the item to them. Sometimes they might make you an offer above your asking price if you agree to sell it to them there and then. The best advice here is to decline politely. Think about it. If they are willing to pay you £20 for something you have listed for £10, it is possible there are people who are willing to match the offer or even go higher. Also remember that if you agree to sell your item 'off eBay' you won't be eligible for protection or help from eBay if the buyer turns out to be a timewaster.

Amending or Adding to Your Item Description

If you receive a question about the item via email, it is possible other people might want to know the same information. You could consider adding the information to your listing. If your item has a bid you can only add information to the View Item in a separate box. If you don't have any bids you are free to edit the item and add or remove anything you want.

You can add to and amend your listing via the 'Services' link in the Navigation Bar.

Tip

The Question and Answer feature can save you time and effort. If you are asked a question by a potential buyer, you can opt to publish the question and your answer on the View Item page. You can do this automatically by selecting the 'Display this question and response on my listing so all buyers can see it' option in the email you receive from eBay.

Cancelling Bids and Blocking Bidders

As the seller you are free to cancel bids for whatever reason you choose. If you don't like a bidder's Feedback you are within your rights to cancel their bids. The bidder is free to bid again and it is polite to inform them that you have cancelled their bid and why.

Don't forget that a bidder with no Feedback isn't necessarily a bad person: it wasn't so long ago that you had no Feedback. Usually a friendly email to a zero-rated bidder will assuage your fears that they aren't bidding in good faith. You can block all buyers who have –1 Feedback or less if you like. You can also ban any buyer who has had a non-payment strike in the last month or who isn't located in a country you are willing to send your item to.

Cancelling bids only removes the bids from one item. In some extreme instances you might want to block a bidder from bidding on any of your items ever again, in which case you can add the bidder to your Blocked Bidder list. This bidder will no longer be able to bid on any of your sales until you remove them from the list. You can add any member to the list regardless of whether they have bid on any of your items or not.

You can Cancel Bids and add members to your Blocked Bidder list using the link on the Services page accessible from the Navigation Bar.

Enjoy It

Many sellers agree that the great excitement of eBay lies in watching the bids come in and seeing the value of your item rise as buyers fight to get their hands on what you're selling. Selling on eBay is addictive: you probably won't be able to stop yourself from checking on your sales as often as possible. So enjoy it!

12 Completing Your Sale

Once your item has ended you will hopefully have a buyer. If you have been successful, you will need to ensure that your buyer has all the information they need to send you their payment. Once you have received payment you are ready to despatch the item and leave your buyer Feedback.

Checkout for Sellers

When you listed your item you had the option to include postage costs for the UK and other locations. If you took a moment to include postage details at that stage, you just need to sit back and wait for the buyer to pay. The buyer has all the details they need to make their payment to you. At the end of the listing they will have received an email and you'll find that many buyers will just pay up without any prompting from you. When they complete Checkout it will be noted for you in My eBay. If they pay by PayPal, you will receive an email notification with the buyer's address. All you need to do is despatch the item.

If they want to pay by cheque or postal order, you will need to wait for it to arrive and, if necessary, clear. eBay will send you an email as soon as the buyer has completed Checkout that will include the buyer's address and any message they have for you. The buyer should then send you payment in the post.

Contact the Buyer

If the buyer doesn't complete Checkout and you don't hear from them, you will need to contact them to make sure everything is OK. Buyers and sellers must contact each other within three days of the listing ending, but a good seller should do it sooner than that and preferably within 24 hours. eBay will have sent you the buyer's contact details in an email at the end of the listing: a quick and friendly email to your buyer will usually do the trick. Sometimes a buyer will need clarification or maybe have a specific request about delivery that you may have to resolve. If they are overseas and you haven't stated a cost for sending the item to their part of the world, you will have to find out the cost before they can pay you. Sometimes the buyer will be new and not know how to complete the purchase, so you may need to be patient and helpful as they find their way.

Whenever you are dealing with a buyer, take the time to communicate clearly. Your buyer doesn't know the person behind the User ID, so make sure your emails do you justice. Most misunderstandings and disagreements on eBay, and online generally, are the result of hastily written emails taken the wrong way.

Despatching the Item

Once your buyer has paid, the ball's in your court: you need to send the buyer the item they have bought and paid for. Where possible you should get the item in the post as quickly as you can. Your buyer shouldn't be kept waiting. Obviously taking a few days is fine, but if a buyer has to wait any longer than that they will often start asking questions. If you can't despatch your item within a few days of receiving cleared payment, you should contact the buyer so they know what to expect. Buyers will typically be very flexible as long as you keep them informed.

It's important to package your item safely and securely. Parcels can get rough treatment as they go through the postal system, so it's best to err on the side of caution when you are judging how well to protect the item. If you are sending your sale overseas, you should pack your item even more securely. If you are sending it outside the EU you will need to fill in a Customs Declaration: you can get these at the post office.

When you do send the item, try to give your parcel the personal touch. Including a pre-printed letter that you have signed is good way of making each and every buyer feel special. Some sellers like to include a personal handwritten note or card. Any note you include should thank the buyer for their purchase and encourage them to leave you positive Feedback. You should also make sure your buyer is in no doubt that they should contact you should they feel moved to leave a negative. This is your chance to connect personally with your buyer and anything you can do to make them feel good about buying from you should be included. You want to encourage repeat buyers and you want to avoid negative Feedback: by coming across as a caring seller you can encourage your buyers to think well of you.

Inside Information:
The Personal Touch

On eBay you are typically buying from other individuals. The experience you so often get on eBay couldn't be more different to buying from a catalogue or ordering from other ecommerce businesses.

Frequently, I get handwritten notes from sellers thanking me for buying the item and hoping I am happy and enjoy it. I bought a video once and the seller enclosed a letter about the film and what he thought about it. I replied with my thoughts after I'd watched it and we exchanged a few emails over the following days. It was nice to have an interesting discussion over email, and this experience isn't unique.

A friend of mine bought a nice piece of jewellery from a lady in Scotland. She wanted to treat herself and she spent about £80 on something she could enjoy wearing. When the item arrived, not only was it better than the seller had described but it had been beautifully packed too. It was like getting a present, said my thrilled friend.

The seller had also included a handwritten letter, explaining that she was an elderly lady selling her jewellery on eBay. She didn't have anyone to leave the items to and she wanted them to find homes where they would be appreciated. She told my friend how she came to own the necklace and she hoped she would get as much enjoyment from owning it as she had.

Another lady I know bought a pair of trousers for her baby daughter on eBay. When they arrived she was surprised to discover that the parcel not only included the trousers but the matching top as well. The seller explained in a note that she hadn't listed the top on eBay because it was slightly soiled, but she thought she would send it anyway because it seemed too good to go in the bin. The top did have a slight mark, but nothing major and certainly not bad enough to warrant chucking it away. My friend was delighted and needless to say left glowing Feedback.

I've heard of sellers who include a sweet or chocolate for the buyer as a treat, but this might be taking it too far. People who include little cards and notes of thanks are commonplace. I've even heard of one seller who includes pictures of her dogs with all her despatches.

Leaving Feedback for Your Buyers

The decision of when to leave Feedback for your buyers is up to you. Many sellers will leave Feedback when they have received cleared payment. The thinking behind this view is that once a buyer has paid in good faith, they have fulfilled their obligations. Other sellers disagree and don't leave Feedback until they get confirmation that the buyer has received the item and is happy with it.

There are no rules when it comes to leaving Feedback for buyers, so you need to decide your own policy. It is true that leaving Feedback first is a good way of ensuring that your buyer reciprocates. If you want to build your eBay Feedback reputation, then it probably makes sense to bite the bullet and leave feedback first.

Inside Information:
Dealing with Difficult Buyers

I've said it before and I'll say it again: the vast majority of people on eBay are good and honest. But some are less than perfect and can be difficult to deal with and you'll have to summon up a bit of patience when they turn up.

The most annoying type of unreliable eBayer is the person who bids but doesn't pay. Obviously you can get your Final Value Fees back, but it's also a pain to chase them and file a dispute. Of the hundreds of sales I have had on eBay I can put my hand on my heart and say that not more than four or five bidders have failed to pay. The most irritating was an American who just couldn't seem to understand that I was located in Britain, that we don't use the dollar over here and that postage from the UK to the US was rather more than from Utah to Oregon. He refused to pay because he was convinced I was trying to fleece him. It was frustrating but thankfully unique in my eBay experience. I prefer to recall the dozens of pleasant and successful trades I've done with our chums in the US.

Then there are the people who are just difficult to please. I had one buyer – whom I eventually refunded when he sent me the item back – who was adamant that the item I despatched wasn't the one I had listed because it looked slightly different in real life to the photograph on eBay. Needless to say, it was one and the same thing. One buyer sent me a snotty email after he received an old 78 rpm record complaining that he was surprised the item had arrived in one piece considering the quality of the packaging. His item had arrived intact and in one piece (as did all the others I sent out), but he just wanted to have a go.

As my mum would say, 'There's just no pleasing some people.' And that's sage advice on eBay. Just stay calm and be polite when you encounter these people and you can't go far wrong.

Unpaid Items

Every now and again a buyer doesn't pay. It's an unfortunate fact of eBay life, but by no means a typical experience. eBay recognises that transactions go awry for all sorts of reasons. Some buyers have a legitimate, if annoying, reason for backing out while others are simply timewasters. The Unpaid Item process means that you can claim back your Final Value Fee for the item that hasn't been paid for. It also alerts eBay that a buyer might be unreliable.

- **File an unpaid item dispute** You can file an Unpaid Item Dispute for up to 45 days after the listing has ended. Sometimes you will know quite quickly if a buyer isn't going to pay. They might tell you they have made a mistake in their bid or that they can't actually afford the item. In these circumstances you can file a dispute immediately. Even if the buyer is from overseas and has sent you payment in the post, you shouldn't expect to wait more than 30 days for payment. Even if you think payment is on the way, it is worth filing a dispute just to be on the safe side. Filing a dispute doesn't mean you have to follow it through: if the buyer pays up you can retract it.

- **Attempt to resolve the dispute** The next step in the process is to communicate with the buyer and attempt to resolve the situation. The ideal resolution is for the buyer to pay up and fulfil their obligation. When you file your dispute the buyer will get an email reminding them to contact you and pay up. Even if they don't want to pay they are encouraged to contact you and explain why. Many buyers do cough up at this point and all is well.

- **Get your Final Value Fee back** If your buyer responds and you are unable to resolve the issue or you don't hear back from them after seven days, you can close the dispute and get your Final Value Fee back. Details of the disputes you have filed are listed in My eBay so you can keep track of them.

- **But it's only a few pence: why bother?** Even if you are only claiming a few pence from eBay when a buyer backs out, it is worth filing an Unpaid Item Dispute because it helps eBay keep an eye on unreliable buyers. If a buyer gets three strikes for non-payment, they will most probably be suspended unless there are significant mitigating circumstances. By claiming back your few pence you are helping other sellers.

You can find complete details about the Unpaid Item process on eBay.co.uk:

http://pages.ebay.co.uk/help/policies/unpaid-item-process.html

• **Minimising unpaid items** There is a useful feature on eBay that can help minimise non-paying bidders: Immediate Payments. On the Sell Your Item form you can choose to require a buyer to pay immediately via PayPal if they win your item. When they bid they have to enter their PayPal details so payment can be taken if they win. This is a good option if you don't want to risk a non-paying bidder, although it does mean that people who don't have PayPal accounts can't bid.

What if My Item Doesn't Sell?

If your item doesn't find a buyer you have two options: give up or have another go. If you want to make money on eBay it's best to have another go, especially if you see similar items to yours selling on the site for a decent price.

• **Consider amending your listing** Is your listing up to scratch? You might need more details or a better picture. Perhaps you could choose a better category or hone the title so your item is easier to find. Cast a critical eye over your listing, because you may well be able to improve it and encourage bidders to make a purchase.

• **Was the price right?** eBayers can be very price sensitive, so it's worth checking that the price you are asking for the item is realistic. Check out other items for sale to gauge whether you are asking over the odds.

• **Relisting your item** You can relist your item on eBay via My eBay. Simply click on the Item Title and you will see a link to relist the item. eBay will walk you through the listing and give you the opportunity to edit and improve it. If your item sells the second time, eBay will refund one set of Listing Fees.

13 Develop Your Selling Skills

Your first selling experiences on eBay will always be the hardest and most nerve-wracking as you will be navigating through unfamiliar territory. But once you have successfully completed your first sale and have mastered the basics of selling on eBay, it will become easier and easier.

You already know how to list a straightforward auction listing, you know about managing your sales and dealing with buyers, and how to despatch the item and ensure you have a happy customer. Once you have mastered these selling basics you'll want to explore the other selling opportunities that eBay offers.

Fixed-Price Selling

You don't have to sell your item by using the auction format. For many, if not all, items, getting buyers to bid against each other is usually the best way to find the fair market value. Lots of buyers like the amusement and drama of bidding and enjoy the search for a bargain. Some people, on the other hand, have neither the time nor the inclination to place bids and wait days for an auction to end: there is no certainty about the price and no guarantee they will win the item. When they see an item they want at an acceptable price, they simply want to buy it now like they would at other online shopping sites. Sometimes they are willing to pay a bit more for the convenience of an instant purchase.

As a seller there are advantages to using a fixed-price option. You have the opportunity to choose a price you will be more than happy to accept for an item you are selling. It also means that you don't have to wait until your auction has ended: if somebody likes your item and buys it, you can get the payment faster and turn the sale around more quickly.

eBay calls this option 'Buy It Now' and as a seller you have two ways of using it. You can either add it to an auction or you can ditch the auction altogether and stage a pure fixed-price Buy It Now listing. Depending on the sort of listing you want, you'll need to make your choice at different stages of the Sell Your Item form.

To add Buy It Now to an auction item you need to choose to sell your item at online auction at the first stage of the Sell Your Item form. You then need to specify the Buy It Now price on the 'Enter Pictures and Item Details' stage of the form. The principles of selling the item are the same. All you need to do is add a higher Buy It Now price. Choosing the price is up to you. Obviously you have a starting price in mind for the item that is the lowest amount you are willing to let the item go for, so your Buy It Now price should be a realistic amount you would be very happy to sell the item for.

If someone bids on your item when you have a Buy It Now option included, it immediately disappears so people can only bid on the item from then on. Adding a Buy It Now option to an auction listing only costs 6p and for the right items in the right situation it can be well worth it.

To use the pure Buy It Now option for a listing you need to express your preference on the first page of the Sell Your Item form. Choose the 'Sell at a Fixed Price' option. You can then list your item as you would normally, choosing a duration and price in the usual way. eBay's fees are determined in the same way as they would be for an auction listing.

Don't forget that you need more than 10 Feedbacks or a direct debit established with eBay before you can use Buy It Now. If you aren't eligible to use pure Buy It Now or to add it to an auction listing, you won't be offered the option to choose it.

Multiple Item Sales

If you have several of the same items you want to sell, you have a number of options available. You can list multiple items in a Buy It Now format, which means buyers can buy as many as they like at a fixed price you choose. The listing stays on the site until all the items have been sold.

You can also utilise the Dutch auction format. This means that bidders can place bids on multiple items and when the listing ends, all the bidders get the items at the lowest possible price.

You can also sell lots on eBay in the same way you might at an old-fashioned auction. To list multiple items, you need to enter the details on the 'Enter Pictures and Item Details' section of the Sell Your Item form.

Turbo Lister

Once you've sold a few items you'll want to build on that success and list more items. If you have the items available, you'll want to sell more than one item at a time. The Sell Your Item form is rather cumbersome when it comes to listing groups of items one after another, especially when so many details in your listings, such as location and payment and postage details, are likely to be either the same or very similar for every listing you create.

eBay has produced a tool called Turbo Lister to help you develop your selling skills. It is a free program that you can download to your computer and use to construct a collection of listings offline and then upload to eBay in one go.

- **What are the benefits of Turbo Lister?** The major benefit of Turbo Lister is that you can create multiple listings offline. This not only saves you money but means that you can come back to your listing and improve and hone it before submitting it to eBay. The other major benefit of Turbo Lister is the feature that means you can reuse details from listing to listing. If you have text that you use in all your listings, then you can save this in Turbo Lister so that it automatically appears in each listing. Payments and postage information can be automatically saved and included in each listing so you will save time.

Turbo Lister also offers you flexibility. If you want to list a collection of items on a Saturday night, you don't need to slave over eBay when you would rather go to the pub. You can create your listings in any spare moment you have during the week and save them on your computer until you want to send them to eBay.

• **When should I start using Turbo Lister?** Turbo Lister is very easy to use so there is no reason why you shouldn't start using it as soon as you want to begin selling more than two or three items at the same time. It is a very convenient way of organising your selling and is suitable even for low-level sellers.

• **Where can I find Turbo Lister?** You can download Turbo Lister to your computer from the link on the Site Map. It is compatible with PC systems and doesn't require very much of your computer space. It is advisable to download the full version even though this might take a while over a 56k connection. It is not compatible with Macs.

14 / eBay's Fees and Rules

Selling Fees

eBay's selling fees can seem complicated to newcomers. Different features and enhancements incur different fees. This section is just a quick overview. The full official fees list can be found on this page: http://pages.ebay.co.uk/help/sell/fees.html.

When you are selling on eBay there are two main types of fees: Listing Fees and Final Value Fees. Listing Fees are payable when you list your item on eBay regardless of whether or not the item sells. These are the fees you incur in the same way you would pay for placing a small ad in a newspaper. If a listing is successful and the item sold to a buyer then you will incur Final Value Fees. This is a percentage fee based on the final price of the item, much like the commission charged when an item is sold at an auction house. The fees stated here are correct at the time of writing, but to get the latest fees consult the eBay site.

Unlike traditional auctioneers eBay has no buyer's premium: only sellers pay eBay fees when an item is sold.

Basic Listing Fees

The Basic Listing Fee charged by eBay is based on the Starting Price of the item. The fees are the same regardless of whether the item is an auction listing or a pure fixed-price Buy It Now sale.

STARTING PRICE OR RESERVE PRICE	FEE
£0.01–0.99	£0.15
£1.00–4.99	£0.20
£5.00–14.99	£0.35
£15.00–29.99	£0.75
£30.00–99.99	£1.50
£100.00 and above	£2.00

If you are listing multiple items in the Multiple Listing format, the Listing Fee payable depends on the total value of all the items collectively rather than the starting price of an individual unit. For instance, if you are selling 10 items worth £4.99 each the listing fee is £1.50 because the collective value is £49.90.

If you list your item in two categories the total Listing Fees are doubled. For scheduled listings an additional 12p is added per listing. If you add Buy It Now to an auction-style listing, there is an additional cost of 6p.

Reserve Prices

If you use a Reserve Price on your item, your Listing Fee will be based not on the Starting Price but the Reserve Price. For instance, if the Starting Price is 1p but the Reserve is £99, the Basic Listing Fee will be £1.50. You can't set a Reserve Price of less than £50.

If you add a Reserve Price you will have to pay a Reserve Price Fee. This is dependent on the Reserve Price you have set. If your Reserve Price is met and the item is sold, your Reserve Price Fee will be refunded.

Listing Enhancements

Listing Enhancements will give your listing greater prominence, but they come at a cost on top of your Basic Listing Fee. Like Basic Listing Fees they are charged regardless of whether or not the item you have listed finds a buyer.

LISTING ENHANCEMENT	FEE
Home Page Featured	£49.95
Featured Plus	£9.95
Highlight	£1.50
Item Subtitle	£0.50
Bold	£0.75
Gallery	£0.15
Featured Gallery	£15.95
Listing Designer Template	£ 0.07

Final Value Fees

If an item is sold Final Value Fees are payable. The Final Value Fee is calculated depending on the final price of your item.

FINAL PRICE RANGE	FINAL VALUE FEE PERCENTAGE
£0–29.99	5.25% for the amount of the sale price up to £29.99
£30.00–599.99	3.25% for the amount of the sale price from £30.00 up to £599.99
£600.00 and up	1.75% for the amount greater than £600.00

So if your item sells for £7, the Final Value Fee will be 5.25% of £7, or 37p. That's simple, but if your item sells for more than £29.99, let's say £50, the Final Value Fee calculation is a little more complex. The amount up to £29.99 is charged at 5.25%; the rest up to £50 is calculated at 3.25%. So that's £1.57 plus 98p, a total of £2.55 on your £50 item.

Find out More

The above examples are correct at the time of writing. All of eBay's fees are inclusive of VAT at 17.5%. If you are VAT registered you can be exempted from paying VAT on your eBay fees. Find out the full details of eBay's fees, including special fees when selling motor vehicles or property, at

http://pages.ebay.co.uk/help/sell/fees.html

Paying Your eBay Fees

eBay offers four ways for you to pay your account. You will be invoiced monthly and expected to pay any balance owed over £1. If you fail to pay your account will be suspended until you do. To find out the balance of your account and how much you owe you should click on the Account link in My eBay.

- **Direct debit** From a seller's point of view the easiest way to pay your eBay fees is by direct debit. When you register as a seller you will be given the option to sign up. All you need to do is print out the direct debit mandate online and eBay will process it. Once your direct debit is established, the amount you owe eBay will be automatically deducted from your bank account on a monthly basis.

- **Credit card on file** Instead of a direct debit you can put your credit card on file for eBay to bill automatically each month. eBay accepts Visa and MasterCard and is totally secure. Some sellers prefer to pay in this way as their payments do not come directly out of their bank accounts.

If you put a credit card on file or establish a direct debit with eBay, you can use the site freely and run up as big a bill as you like. Otherwise eBay provides a £15 trading limit for all members. If you are going to be using eBay but are unlikely to run up more than £15 a month, you might prefer to use the pay-as-you-go options offered. Don't forget, though, that if you exceed the £15 limit your account will be blocked from selling until you have paid off the balance.

- **PayPal** If you want to pay as you go, then using PayPal is quick and easy. Your payment will be applied instantly to your account and you can use the money you have received from buyers to settle your bill. If you don't have money in your account you can use your credit or debit card via PayPal to settle your bill. You will find the link to pay eBay using PayPal on the Accounts section of My eBay.

- **One-time credit card payment** If you don't have a PayPal account you can make a one-time credit card payment. You can do this via My eBay in the same way as you would using PayPal.

• **Cheque** The slowest and most inconvenient way to pay is by cheque. You will need to print out a payment slip and send the cheque in the post. It can take up to 15 working days for eBay to process your payment. You can access this option via the Accounts tab in My eBay.

eBay's Selling Rules

Being familiar with eBay's rules is vital if you want to make money on eBay. If you break a rule then eBay will remove your listing from the site, which is not only a pain but it means that all the time and effort you invested in creating the listing will be wasted.

Things You Can't Sell on eBay

You can sell almost anything on eBay, but obviously there are certain things that eBay doesn't permit to be listed. Some items are prohibited because it is illegal to trade in them, and some are banned because eBay has taken a pragmatic stand or because the items are heavily regulated and it would be impossible for eBay to keep track.

• **Guns, knives, bootlegs, drugs and pornography** Firearms, illegal weapons, illegal drugs, prescription drugs and tobacco are all banned pretty much without exception, as are bootlegs and copies of recordings. You should also avoid selling anything pornographic or adult in nature (and that means no top-shelf magazines). Even items that are listed featuring nude or bare-breasted women in an adult way are likely to be ended if they are listed on eBay.co.uk.

• **Body parts, animals and plants** You can't sell human body parts or items fashioned from human body parts (apart from whole skeletons for medical research purposes as long as they have the requisite licences). There are also rules restricting the listing of animal skins, furs or pelts, birds' eggs and ivory. You aren't allowed to sell any animal that is alive (except the rare exception of some live pet foods and fish), although plants and seeds are generally permitted as long as they aren't marijuana.

- **Alcohol** You cannot sell alcoholic drinks on eBay unless you have the appropriate licence and eBay's express permission. Alcohol can be listed, however, if the bottle or container is collectable in its own right and more sought after than the contents.

- **Embargoed goods** eBay.co.uk is a subsidiary of an American company, which means that listing Cuban items is generally not allowed. There are also prohibitions on items that come from countries against which the UK has an embargo.

- **'Hate items'** There are restrictions applied to what eBay calls 'hate' items. You can't list items that bear the Nazi swastika or the SS lightning motif. Other World War Two items are generally permissible. Items related to the Ku Klux Klan or mass murderers are also restricted.

- **How does eBay know if I am selling prohibited or restricted items?** eBay has a very effective policing system in place: all the other buyers and sellers. If a member sees an item that is not permitted for sale there is a strong chance they will report it to eBay. For some sellers it is a great way to eliminate competition, but for others it is simply a way of keeping eBay safe. The eBay community is very passionate about preserving its marketplace.

- **What will eBay do if it finds out I am selling restricted items?** eBay takes a very dim view of sellers who break the rules and attempt to sell prohibited items. If you do list an item that is prohibited or restricted and it is your first offence, eBay will probably just end the item, refund your fees and give you a warning. If you continue to break the rules you will be suspended and banned from the site.

This list isn't comprehensive and the list of banned and regulated items on eBay changes frequently. You can find eBay's full and up-to-date list here:

http://pages.ebay.co.uk/help/sell/item_allowed.html

Things You Can't Include in Your Listing

The listing policies that exist govern what can and cannot be included in an item listing. Every seller is bound by these policies and failure to follow them can result in a warning from eBay. If you continue to violate the policies, eBay will suspend you from the site and you will no longer be able to buy or sell on it.

Most of the policies are straightforward and make perfect sense, although some are complex. This is only a summary of the most important policies. For full details of the listing policies, which are updated occasionally, visit:

http://pages.ebay.co.uk/help/policies/ia/listing_policies_for_sellers.html

> • **Links policy** There are strict policies governing the links you can include in your listing. You may not have links to other websites unless they are credits or links for payment services, photographs or further details about the item for sale. Any link that encourages buyers to leave eBay and purchase items elsewhere is not allowed. You can include links to your other eBay listings, your About Me page and your eBay Shop.

> • **Choice listings, bonuses, giveaways and prizes** When you list an item on eBay you must be listing a specific item and that item alone. You cannot offer a choice between different items. For instance, if you have two identical pairs of shoes and one pair is green and the other is red, you cannot list them as a single auction and give the buyer the option to buy the red or green pair when the listing ends. You would have to list a green pair of shoes or a red pair or both separately. You are not allowed to offer prizes or giveaways as an enticement to buy from you. You can offer a bonus item as long as the bonus is available to all buyers alike.

> • **Surcharges** It is normal practice for sellers to pass on the postage and handling costs to their buyer. However, these must be reasonable and stated up front where possible. Sellers should not profit from postage costs. Escrow fees can also be passed on to the buyer as can currency conversion costs, as long as they are disclosed in advance and agreed to by the buyer.

You may not pass on the cost of taking online payments when using a service such as PayPal. If you are processing credit card payments using your own merchant service, you are permitted to charge a surcharge to cover your costs. Under eBay's rules the credit card surcharge must not exceed the costs of receiving or processing the payment and can only be passed on to buyers in the UK trading in pounds sterling.

• **Keyword spamming** You are not allowed to include irrelevant words in your Item Title so that it gets more attention from the Search facility. For instance, if you are selling a Swatch watch you are not permitted to list it as 'Swatch not Rolex' so that more people find it when searching.

• **Fee avoidance** Obviously eBay isn't keen on any feature of a listing that means that the seller is avoiding its selling fees. You are not allowed to list an item with a very low price but very high postage so you can avoid fees but not lose money. You are also not allowed to list an item for a low price but say in the listing that the price will in fact be much higher.

• **Other rules** You are not allowed to post want ads on eBay. Any listing that includes profanity or is adult or erotic in nature will be ended. All items should be listed in an appropriate category and you are not permitted to list more than 10 identical items at any one time unless you are using the Multiple Listing format.

PART III

MAKING SERIOUS MONEY: BECOME AN eBAY EXPERT

15 / Create an About Me Page

When you are selling items on eBay you are not just selling your products: you are also selling yourself as a good person to trade with. You need to inspire trust in buyers, so you should use every opportunity available to you. One tool that many sellers overlook is the About Me page.

What to Include on an About Me Page

A member's About Me page does exactly what it says on the packet: it's your chance to tell the rest of the eBay community all about yourself. At the most basic level you can use your About Me page to talk about your passions, interests, activities on eBay and general information about who you are. But as you start selling you can use it as a valuable part of your reputation as a seller.

- **Build trust with your About Me page** As you decide what you want to include on your About Me page, don't forget the purpose you are building it for: to get an edge on your competitors and come across as *the* person a buyer wants to trust and buy from. This of course doesn't mean you need to be stuffy or formal; you simply need to present details that cast you in a good light.

  Be real and don't pretend to be something you aren't. If you do you'll just seem like a fake and no one will trust you.

Coming across as a real person will benefit you more than trying to sound like a business or corporation.

Many sellers like to include funny stories, pictures and details about themselves. But be careful not to give too much away. There are people out there who might want to misuse personal information, so protect your privacy.

• **News and updates** If you are selling items on eBay, your About Me page is an ideal place to make useful information available to buyers. For instance, if you can only make it to the post office twice a week on Wednesday and Saturday, then you can note it here for your buyers.

If you have a holiday coming up or plan to take a few months off eBay selling, then putting it on your About Me page helps buyers make decisions. Also, if you have similar or complementary items you plan to be selling in a few weeks' time, you can encourage buyers to come back and check out your sales by telling them in advance here.

• **Your selling policies** Your About Me page is also a great place to lay out how you do business. Obviously you'll want to include some of this information in your item listings, but it doesn't do any harm to make information common to all your listings available on your About Me page too.

• **Postage terms** If you prefer to send your items using insured methods such as recorded or registered delivery, you can note that on your About Me page for all your buyers to see.

• **Refunds and returns** Many sellers note the circum-stances under which they will accept a return and offer a refund. The benefit of putting this on your About Me page is that you don't need to clog up your listings with too much detail. You can simply have a link in your listing that says 'Click here for my refunds and returns policy'.

• **Keep it up to date** It shouldn't take you too long to decide what to include on your About Me page, but once it is live on the site make sure you update it every now and again to ensure it is current and helping you to win over buyers.

How to Build an About Me Page

To create an About Me page write the text in a Word document before you even log on. You can find the link to create an About Me page on the site map and in My eBay.

The easiest way to build the page is to use one of the ready-made templates that eBay provides free of charge. If you use one of the templates you can simply choose a layout you like and copy and paste your pre-prepared text into the fields provided. You don't need to be familiar with HTML: you can style the text to the way you select using the edit functions.

If you want to include pictures you can, but you'll need to host the images on your own webspace and paste the image location or URL into the page. You can also include links to your favourite websites. If you know HTML and would prefer to start from scratch and make a truly individual About Me page, that is perfectly possible.

16 / Make eBay Work for You

Once you have bought and sold items you have mastered the basics of eBay. You have the essential skills required to use the site safely and with confidence. Whatever you decide to do on eBay will now merely be a variation on what you already know: you have all the know-how to make serious money.

On your travels around the site you may have seen PowerSellers or people with a huge amount of Feedback. These people have taken their eBay activity to the next level and have made eBay a part of their lives. The opportunities eBay provides are not confined to striking out and forming your own company. You might just want a comfortable second income that could fund an extra-special holiday or help you buy a better car. How you use eBay is up to you: there are a wealth of opportunities for making money.

Inside Information: Supplementing Your Income

Over the years I've worked for eBay, I've been amazed by the huge variety of ways people use it to make money. I started selling in my final terms at university to take the burden off my already tight finances. I didn't really want to get a job that didn't fit with my studies, and eBay allowed me huge flexibility because I could use the site as and when I wanted. Even now I like to sell items regularly to make a bit of extra money.

I've met people who use eBay as a sideline to their day job or to help them through a lean patch. I met one lady who found she was always short of a few quid by the end of the month, so two weeks ahead of payday she started her sales so that in the days before her salary was paid she wasn't totally broke. She simply sold clothes and accessories that she already had to help herself out. I didn't have the heart to suggest to her that if she were only more disciplined about buying such luxuries at the start of the month she wouldn't need eBay.

I reckon that if you put your mind to it, you can easily make £100 profit a month using eBay. And if you get organised – and you will need to be organised – you shouldn't need to spend more than eight hours a month making the extra money. I've met dozens of people who do this month in, month out. It's a great little extra income that doesn't require a huge outlay.

But £100 isn't a limit: you can make much more money than that if you want to. Some people have managed to build small businesses by selling on eBay. And of course, there are people who make hundreds of thousands of pounds annually too.

eBay as a Great Money-Making Hobby

Starting off slowly is probably the best advice: if you decide eBay is for you then you can take it further. For lots of people eBay is a stimulating, money-making hobby.

Audrey is a pensioner who likes to keep active and discover new things. After taking a 'Computing for the Terrified' course she was keen to become a fully fledged silver surfer and discover what the internet had to offer. Her tutor introduced the class to eBay and Audrey quickly got down to buying additions for her various collections. As a fan of Spode and Worcester porcelain, she found eBay the perfect place to indulge her passion. She also started selling items she didn't want any more, enjoying not merely the money she made but also her new hobby. She likes the eBay Discussion Boards and the lively chats and people she encounters there.

On a typical day Audrey is out scouring junk shops, charity shops and jumble sales for things to sell on eBay. She particularly enjoys the sociability of her expeditions and delights in telling her friends about her latest successful sale; she has already converted some of her friends to the site.

Once a week she photographs her booty and fires up Turbo Lister to put the items up for sale. She starts all her listings off at a penny and loves watching the bids come in. She says that even though the money comes in handy, she sells on eBay because it keeps her active and she likes talking to her buyers all over the world: she has struck up cyber-friendships with buyers in Australia and America via eBay and corresponds with them regularly. Her best sale was a 10p plate she found at a jumble sale, which she sold for more than £50 to a collector in Toronto.

eBay Selling as a Second Income

Tina is a mother of three who planned to return to her job at a supermarket after the birth of her youngest child. She needed to supplement the household income and part-time work was the only option, even though she didn't like leaving her children and childcare costs were expensive.

A friend recommended eBay as a great place to buy baby clothes and toys for her children at a good price. Before long Tina was selling all her unneeded baby clothes and toys to make a bit of extra money. Her selling was so successful that she started looking around her local shops for other things to sell.

eBay made her life easier. Instead of having to go out to work she now supplements the household income from home with hours that suit her and her role as a housewife and mother. Trips to the post office and bank can easily be slotted around taking the children to school and she enjoys corresponding with her customers, who are typically other mums.

Tina is particularly proud of one of her recent sales. She bought 10 Harry Potter school bags at a local bargain shop for £3 each. She was astonished to discover how much they fetched on eBay: £30 each. She says, 'It certainly beats working behind the checkouts.'

eBay for Existing Businesses

eBay isn't only about people who want to build a business from scratch. Many people use it as an additional sales channel to breathe new life into an existing business.

Robert has been in the stamp trade for 30 years. He runs a shop on the South Coast and regularly attends fairs up and down the country. After several tough years he was considering leaving the business he loves, until he discovered eBay and used it to boost his previously dwindling profits.

Robert says that trade had been getting harder, with increasing rents and the other expenses he incurred running his shop and attending events. He thought he would give eBay a try, although he wasn't hopeful. When he listed his first items for sale he fully expected to be disappointed. He chose to begin with some unexciting Commonwealth stamps that had been in his shop unsold for a number of years. He was pleasantly surprised when he not only sold the stamps but found they reached nearly twice as much as he expected.

Robert was so impressed that he set about listing all the hard-to-shift stock he had kept in the back room of his shop. Stuff that he had previously believed he would never sell was being snapped up by philatelists all over the world. His experiment in eBay selling has proved so successful that he is considering closing his shop and concentrating full-time on selling his stamps on eBay.

Building an eBay Business

Barry was already contemplating a career change when he discovered eBay. Having worked in the public sector for many years, he was keen to start a business and become his own boss, but he wasn't sure where to begin. No stranger to technology, he realised that eBay would be a great way to sell parts and accessories for computers. He was attracted to the prices such items got on eBay when compared to specialist shops, and because the items are typically small and light they would not be difficult or costly to send to buyers. Most importantly, he didn't need a great deal of capital and simply began operating out of his garage.

After a very successful start, Barry realised he could use the skills he had acquired and his knowledge of the eBay marketplace to diversify the items he sold and build his business. He established relationships with wholesale sellers and sold digital cameras and mobile phone accessories alongside his other sales. His wife has been able to give up her job as a school secretary to help him run the business.

Barry ascribes the success of his business to his personal service and cross-selling. He takes the time to offer a genuine and human service that people don't get from retailers. He is very conscious that many people buying computer items are not experts. By helping them get what they really need he has established a glowing feedback record and numerous repeat buyers, who look to him first when they need to get their hands on a computer-related item.

Cross-selling has been critical to his success. If a customer buys a camera, he'll let them know that he can also supply cases and memory cards at a competitive price using eBay's cross-selling tools, and will reduce his postage costs if they take the plunge and purchase an additional item.

After only a year Barry has achieved Gold PowerSeller status and his business has a monthly turnover of thousands of pounds. But best of all, Barry is his own boss and is still able to work from home.

Fact: eBay estimates that nearly half a million people make a living on the site in the USA.

17

eBay PowerSelling

While you've been buying and selling on eBay you might have seen a PowerSeller logo beside some sellers' User IDs. A PowerSeller is someone who has been recognised by eBay for their high level of sales. Naturally, eBay wants to retain high-volume sellers and the PowerSeller programme is a sort of loyalty scheme that encourages them to keep on trading.

Inside Information:
PowerSellers

PowerSellers are an important part of the eBay community. Not only do they make up a significant proportion of listings on the site, in many ways they set the tone for how other members trade. Of course there are PowerSellers who push the rules to breaking point and give the others a bad name, but generally they are good people making an honest living on eBay.

It isn't an exclusive club. If you are serious about selling on eBay, reaching the minimum level of £750 a month shouldn't be difficult. But if you want to make a living you need to shift a great deal more stock than that!

Nevertheless, it is possible. Over the years I have met dozens of PowerSellers and most of them are people who took a punt and succeeded. You don't need a business degree or even a GCSE to be a PowerSeller: you simply need to sell things. I've met former cab drivers who have chucked that in to sell event tickets. There's one guy who does very well selling vintage sewing machines to America. There's a lovely lady near Bristol who sells equestrian items to fund her expensive dressage habit. There is a couple in Liverpool who have set up an international business selling postal supplies to other eBayers.

While it isn't easy, anyone can do it. All you need is to research your market, have something to sell and put the hours in. Before long you'll be an expert in postal rates and packing material, but you will also be your own boss. That's the attraction for so many PowerSellers: eBay has given them the opportunity to strike out on their own and do something they never dreamed they could.

What Is a PowerSeller?

A PowerSeller is a seller who meets a set of minimum criteria laid down by eBay. First, they must maintain a certain level of monthly sales: to qualify you must sell a minimum of £750 worth of goods a month or 100 items.

But just having a good month isn't enough. A PowerSeller must maintain their sales for three consecutive months in order to qualify. They must also make up those sales from more than four listings a month: selling a £1000 car each month for three months won't work.

However, PowerSelling isn't merely about selling lots of stuff. It's about being a good eBay citizen and having excellent Feedback. PowerSellers have a minimum Feedback of 100 and must maintain a 98% positive rating and also be professional, diligent and trustworthy. Breaking eBay's rules or getting a bunch of negative Feedback is the fast track to losing PowerSeller status. They must keep their eBay account in good standing and pay their fees, as well as be sure to contact buyers within three days of the end of a listing. And beware, eBay doesn't make exceptions for PowerSellers. Being a PowerSeller is something of an honour and it doesn't buy any exemptions.

There are five different level of PowerSeller: Bronze, Silver, Gold, Platinum and Titanium. Each level requires a minimum level of monthly sales:

Bronze	£750
Silver	£1500
Gold	£6000
Platinum	£15000
Titanium	£95000

Different PowerSeller levels offer different benefits and there is great competition to move up the ranks and join the increasingly more exclusive groups. There is only a handful of Titanium PowerSellers in Britain. You can also qualify as a PowerSeller by selling a minimum number of items on the site. If you are listing hundreds of low-value items every month, which don't take you to the minimum sales threshold, you might also qualify.

Being a PowerSeller isn't a lifelong club: to maintain PowerSeller status you must keep selling the minimum amounts each month and maintain a good Feedback level too. If you fail to meet the criteria you will be given a warning before being removed from the PowerSeller programme.

How Do I Become a PowerSeller?

If you meet the criteria you will automatically qualify, you don't need to apply. eBay contacts new PowerSellers every month with details of how they can take advantage of the service. You can check whether you are eligible by visiting the PowerSeller pages, which can be accessed from the Site Map.

What Are the Benefits of Being a PowerSeller?

The higher the PowerSeller level, the greater the benefits. All levels of PowerSeller are permitted to use the PowerSeller logo in their listings and also in any promotional material they produce. For instance, many PowerSellers take pride in including the logo on their business cards and letterheads. A lot of PowerSellers say that the logo is the best perk of the programme: it shows buyers that the seller is professional and bound by special rules. This inspires others to bid with confidence.

All PowerSeller levels are eligible for invitations to PowerSeller events (such as meetings with eBay staff and master-classes in eBay selling with experts) and have access to a dedicated PowerSeller Discussion Board to meet and talk with others about eBay selling. Every PowerSeller has access to priority customer support via email and can expect a response in super-quick time. PowerSellers can also expect advice and troubleshooting on how to develop their business.

Gold-level PowerSellers and above also have access to customer support on the telephone. During business hours they can reach a member of the customer support team dedicated to PowerSellers' needs. This is ideal for high-volume sellers who have a complex query that might be difficult to resolve via email. PowerSellers can also enjoy preferential rates from Paypal: the higher the level the lower the fees.

PowerSellers and the Rules

If anything, as a PowerSeller you are under more pressure to abide by eBay's rules. If one PowerSeller does break them you will find that other PowerSellers, keen to protect the value of the PowerSeller programme, will report that seller to eBay. Buyers will also expect more from a PowerSeller and they are open to greater scrutiny and more attention than other sellers.

PowerSellers don't get any special treatment from eBay. They will be warned and sanctioned like any other member. It really pays to be aware of the rules and follow them. After all, if they do break them they have a lot more to lose than most members.

10 Steps to Successful PowerSelling

There is no great secret to becoming a PowerSeller on eBay. Unfortunately, there is no single piece of information that will make it easy or give you the fast track to success. However, you can be sure it won't be a walk in the park. Building a business on eBay takes hard graft in the same way that building a traditional business does, but the rewards are potentially huge. eBay offers you a unique and enormous market that is not available anywhere else: you will have access to over 120 million customers.

More than 10,000 people in Britain are already eBay PowerSellers. Many of them are making a full-time living, running their businesses purely on the site. Most don't have shops or

outlets and they don't sell their items anywhere else. It's astonishing to note that very few were businesspeople before they
started off. Many are ordinary people just like you and me who
saw a great opportunity and grasped it.

If you are ready to join the ranks of the eBay PowerSellers,
you'll have to prepare and plan. Everyone who is a successful
seller on eBay has found their own path and probably made some
mistakes along the way too. Here are some things to think about.

Become an eBay Expert

First and foremost, you are going to need to know eBay inside
out. Learn the rules and policies. What could be worse than planning your business and investing in thousands of pounds worth of
Cuban cigars, only to discover that eBay won't let you sell them?
(Which as we have seen it doesn't.) Take the time now so you
don't waste money later.

Learn the listing policies too. You can't list more than 10
identical items, for instance, unless you use a multiple item listing
format. eBay won't cut you any slack just because you are a
PowerSeller. When it comes to the rules, it enforces them across
the board.

Discover how eBay works and get a feel for its procedures
and oddities. Don't forget to experiment with selling to make sure
it's right for you. Buy items on eBay to see how other sellers run
their business.

Find Your Market

The easiest way to succeed on eBay is to find a niche. If you can
identify something that lots of people want to buy but no one else
is selling on eBay, you've cracked it. Needless to say, that isn't as
easy as it sounds. With hundreds and thousands of sellers out
there, the chances are that someone else is already doing what
you're planning. But don't let that discourage you.

Perhaps you can surf a current trend or even predict one. If
you can get your hands on a product that is going to be the next
big thing, you're on to a winner. I know a number of people who
simply bought up lots of Harry Potter Lego and waited until it
was scarce and unavailable in the shops. That Christmas it was
the must-have gift, and they were quids in. But more often than
not this is a one-off and difficult to do again and again to make a

living. However, by keeping your eyes open you'll soon get a feel for what's going to sell well on eBay.

If you can't find a niche, don't worry. You can offer goods cheaper than other people and do it with greater panache. Buyers on eBay value the extra mile sellers go to make their purchases pleasant and trouble free. Describe your items more fully. Take better pictures. Make yours the items people want to buy and compete with existing sellers already. If you can stand out from the crowd and make people notice you, customers will buy from you.

The best advice is to sell something you are knowledgeable about and comfortable with. Utilise experience you already have to attract buyers. Equally, don't be afraid to experiment and do something a bit different. A lot of people sell original craftwork and paintings. If you have a hobby or skill, consider whether you can produce things that other people want.

Sort out Supply

You will need to ensure that you have a ready source of inventory if you want to succeed. You can't sell stuff you don't have. How to get stuff to sell in sufficient quantities at a price where you can still make a profit is a very real challenge that every PowerSeller faces.

You want a supply of items that meets your capacity as a seller; that is, a quantity of inventory that will keep you going and make money. Build a relationship with a supplier who can provide you with a regular supply of goods. Lots of PowerSellers have multiple suppliers so that when one supply falls through they are not left in the lurch.

One source of supply you might consider is eBay itself. Many wholesale sellers list pallets and lots that they don't have the capacity to sell themselves. If you can take the time to break the lots down and sell them on, you might be on to a winner. Buying some of these lots from the Wholesale category can also be a great way of starting on eBay.

Buy your stock at a price that ensures you have a good profit margin. It's an obvious point, but one that many people don't consider. You can sell 100 things for £10 each, but if you are only making £1 a time you are going to need to sell a fair few to make a living. Of course it's not impossible, but it's better either to find something with a bigger margin or to sell more expensive items with the same percentage margin.

Don't forget to factor your time in to your costs. Selling can be time consuming. It's going to be a bit galling looking over your sales for the month and realising that you would have been better off behind the checkout at your local supermarket earning the minimum wage.

Get Organised

You'll need to be an efficient selling machine to make it big on eBay. It's about getting the nuts and bolts of your business in place. For instance, you are going to have to become an expert in postal rates. You are also going to need a cheap and reliable supplier of packaging material. The best place to buy padded envelopes and other supplies like this is, needless to say, on eBay. Check out the costs and ensure you factor them into your selling prices.

Make sure you are organised and can receive payments from your buyers. Giving customers a choice is the key. As a minimum you should be prepared to accept PayPal, cheques, postal orders and bank transfers. Be certain you are ready.

Don't forget the legal stuff too. You might need to become VAT registered if you are going to be shifting a fair bit of stock. It might pay to become a registered business. Many banks get a little tricky when it comes to taking lots of cheque payments if you don't have a business account. If you are going to be trading overseas you'll need to be up to speed on Customs and Excise procedures. Did you know that when you export items from the UK you can expedite the process by ensuring what you are sending has the appropriate customs TARIC code on it? If not, you can find out more from the website www.hmce.co.uk.

Build Your Brand and Market Yourself

Successful sellers on eBay don't just sell products, they sell themselves. A key part of your success will be about how you identify yourself and how you develop your brand. Your brand is essentially what you say about yourself, how you promote yourself and what people think of you. It's the personality of your business. For instance, a brand such as Gap is about being young, trendy and energetic. Harrods banks more on being a classy, old-fashioned and exclusive brand. You need to decide how you brand yourself.

Some eBay sellers position themselves as high-quality pur-
veyors with an eye on personal service. This will suit an antiques
dealer who provides very detailed descriptions and sells expensive items. Others prefer a more jokey brand and sometimes
create a persona for their business with a fictional character.
Some appeal to the bargain hunters and go for a 'pile it high, sell
it cheap' style. Whatever you decide, it should be a part of everything you do.

The first element must be your User ID. It should be recog-
nisable and related to your selling activities. Random selections
of letters and numbers or something obscure or oblique won't do.
You need an ID that is catchy and memorable. You can also
express your brand on eBay by the colour schemes you use in
your listings and when you communicate with buyers. You might
want to invent a slogan. Check out other PowerSellers to see how
they do it. If you are serious about taking your PowerSelling to
the next level, it might be worth checking out whether your
chosen User ID is the name of an existing company, because this
could well save you bother in the long run.

Don't forget to create an About Me page with information
for buyers about you and your business, because this helps both
to build trust and drive sales. Tell buyers about how you trade,
your returns policies and aims. Some sellers include a profile of
themselves and a picture to reassure buyers that they are dealing
with another human being rather than an uncaring corporation.

Exploit eBay's Features

eBay wants sellers to be successful and the facilities for sellers
are not limited to the auction format. Don't forget that you can
use the Buy It Now fixed-price option or multiple listing formats,
which are great if you have lots of identical items you want to
shift.

You might want to open an eBay shop, a way of utilising
eBay technology to create your own ecommerce store. So if you
have a website and you want to include your eBay sales, a shop
might be just the ticket.

It's a matter of horses for courses and obviously not all features will be useful to all sellers. You'll need to experiment and
explore what works for you and your business.

Know Your Enemies

Keep an eye on what other sellers are doing, especially if they are competitors. Not only will you be able to emulate what they are doing well, you can learn from their mistakes. Some PowerSellers even have secondary accounts so they can buy items from competitors without them knowing. This way you have a full picture of how a competitor trades and you can strive to do better. (You're allowed to have as many eBay accounts as you like, so it's perfectly possible to do a bit of customer intelligence gathering.)

eBay buyers are very price conscious and through undercutting your competitors, even by a little, you will attract sales. Don't forget to be competitive on postage costs too. If you can offer cheaper shipping costs, you are at an advantage.

Know Your Limits

Don't overstretch yourself. There's very little point in being wildly successful and raking in lots of cash if you can't enjoy it. Too often you hear of PowerSellers who are shifting hundreds of items a month and making a healthy profit on them – they have never had more disposable income and yet they have never had less time to enjoy it. Schedule days off and holidays too.

But there is a serious business point here as well. A PowerSeller who is working at capacity, selling, packing, emailing customers and sourcing supply, doesn't have time to think. It's too easy to neglect the big picture when you are lost in a sea of Jiffy bags and brown tape. It's too easy to lose control and fail to notice where you can maximise your profit and develop your business.

Many PowerSellers work in partnership with their spouses, dividing up the work between them. Or if you need to get a willing employee in for a few hours a week to package up your sales, it could be worthwhile. The hours you save can be usefully spent either analysing your business or seeking out new sources of supply. They will give you time out to enjoy yourself and think about your business.

Never Forget Your Customers

Your customers are the key to your success: never take them for granted. You can get everything else right, but if you neglect the people who are buying your stuff you will fail. Many PowerSellers say that the most valuable customers are repeat customers. You should strive to offer every customer a seamless and easy transaction.

In many ways it's all about being prompt, polite and responsive. Buyers love a swift turnaround on their purchases and will often provide glowing feedback if they receive their item super-quick. Consider including a note with your despatches. It can be pre-printed and simply signed, but it does make every buyer feel looked after.

Buyers also love flexibility and personal service, so try to be open to their requests. It may only take a minute or two but you'll reap the rewards when they come back to you to buy again.

Improve, Evolve, Adapt, Develop

Once you are successful on eBay you can't merely sit on your laurels. Here's a cautionary tale. There once was a very successful PowerSeller who was getting it right and raking it in. He had never earned so much money before in his life. He cornered a market and was the most prolific and profitable seller in his category. But one day he noticed that there was another seller in his category, challenging his supremacy. He was outraged that someone should try to invade his ground.

As he saw his sales slip away, he refused to take advice and improve his selling techniques. He had thousands of sales under his belt so he couldn't possibly be doing anything wrong, he thought. Everything was at fault but him. He blamed eBay. It was going to the dogs, he said. He claimed there was no money to be made on the site any more. He quit eBay selling and went back to his previous business.

His competitor is still thriving. He is now the biggest seller in the category, making more money each and every month. He does it by watching how the category develops and adapting his sales to compete effectively. He thrives on the competition and is confident he can provide the items buyers want at a price they like. But he isn't arrogant enough to assume there isn't any room for improvement.

To succeed on eBay you have to be nimble and flexible. You will need to reassess the competition frequently, stay on your toes and make sure you compete with the ever-changing market. This shouldn't be scary but refreshing instead. If you get stuck in your ways, you will fail. Constantly improve your listings. Evolve your business and adapt your approach to eBay selling. If you don't develop you'll soon become a dinosaur. And look what happened to them.

18 / Trading Safely on eBay

This is the most important chapter of the book. eBay is a great way to make money and find bargains, but there is also a very low level of fraud on the site. The best way to protect yourself is to get tooled up with the information you need.

Buying Safely

One of eBay's core values is the belief that people are basically good. And for the most part the truth of this maxim is borne out in the everyday trading activities of eBay members all over the world. People are trading all the time with people they have never met, sending money to strangers and receiving items in return that they have not seen or handled before. eBay is based on trust and the vast majority of purchases and sales go without a hitch, leaving both buyers and sellers satisfied.

Despite the many good and decent people out there, it is nevertheless the sad truth that some people set out to do bad things. eBay has systems in place to detect such people, punish them and remove them from the marketplace, but you can protect yourself further by being vigilant. Your greatest tool to avoid being one of the people who gets ripped off is your own common sense.

Inside Information:
The 'Man in the Pub' Rule

If you wouldn't take a risk in real life, you shouldn't do it online either. For instance, imagine a man you'd never met before came up to you in the pub and said he would sell you the Harley Davidson you had always dreamt of owning for £5000. You wouldn't give that man £5000 there and then and wait until he returned with the bike, would you?

You would want to ensure you were protected, verify the bike was real and confirm that it was exactly what you wanted. Most likely you wouldn't hand over the money until you collected it. That's just common sense. The same principle applies on eBay.

I can't make this point strongly enough: using your common sense when trading on eBay will ensure that you stay safe. If a seller wants you to pay using a service you aren't comfortable with or have never heard of, don't use it. Someone who wants to rip you off doesn't want you to pay using a secure service such as PayPal. If they attach odd terms and conditions such as using a particular escrow service other than escrow.com, eBay's recommended escrow partner, you should be wary. Especially with high-value items, make sure you can get your money back if you need to.

Over the years I've seen a number of people ripped off or scammed on eBay, but it still represents an astonishingly small percentage of the total transactions that occur worldwide. What makes me angry is that fact that most scams like these are totally avoidable if you take a moment to engage your common sense before you get out your wallet.

Feedback

Feedback is your greatest tool in deciding whether a certain seller or buyer is the kind of person you want to do business with. The Seller Information Box on the Item Description page gives you plenty of information at a glance.

You should make sure that the location of the seller tallies with the location of the item and that the positive percentage of Feedback is up to scratch. Look for a positive Feedback score of

98% or above. Remember that a high total isn't automatically a guarantee in itself. If you want to find out about a seller, or if you are curious about a buyer, you should click on the Feedback total to find out more about their eBay history.

The Member Profile gives you much more detail about a member's previous activities on eBay and will give you more information with which to form a judgement. If there is any negative Feedback on the profile you will want to find out what it is for. A person with 1000 Feedbacks has clearly had many successful trades with many different members, but a closer examination will reveal if a trader has received complaints. A few negative Feedbacks here and there are pretty much inevitable for members with a lot of Feedback, but sometimes even excellent Feedback totals conceal members with less than enviable reputations.

If you are looking into a seller you can check the items they have sold recently and examine the Feedback left. If a seller has already received good Feedback for an item similar to the one you want to bid on, then you can probably bid with confidence.

The clues are there

There is no universal factor that will reveal a dodgy listing on eBay, but there are certain clues to look out for when you are bidding and buying. Obviously, some areas are more risky than others: mobile phones, plasma screen televisions and other electrical goods are prone to attracting fraudsters more than, say, stamps or Beanie Babies. If you keep an eye out for the following features in listings then you will be safer.

If a listing has standard pictures and descriptions of an item cribbed from other websites, it is worth asking yourself why. For many sellers it is a quick and simple way of constructing a listing, but it also a hallmark of fraudulent sellers who copy descriptions and pictures from official websites. Obviously, they don't have the items to photograph and describe, so they have to rely on information already in the public domain.

Avoid sellers with restricted payment terms. Does the listing insist on wire transfer or payment by Western Union? Beware of sellers who want to use untrackable payment methods, especially if they are located outside the UK. Be careful as well if the seller is registered in one country and the item is located in a different country. Beware of sellers who might want you to send money to a different country while claiming to be located in the UK. Fraudsters can be found all over the world, but on eBay be especially careful and secure when sending payment to Indonesia, the Ukraine or Romania, where criminal gangs are active.

Make sure you read the small print. One scam you sometimes see is a listing that looks as though it is selling a mobile phone at an impossibly low price. When you read the description carefully you will see that what is really on offer is a link that will show you where to buy the phone at a discount price, rather than the phone itself.

Keep an eye out for sellers who have changed their habits recently or have started selling different items from usual. One trick favoured by fraudsters is the account takeover. This is where a seller is tricked into giving away their personal details and their account is then hijacked and used to sell fraudulent items. The fraudsters use the good Feedback and reputation of the honest seller to shield their activities. This is why it can be wise to go through some of the items a seller has sold recently to get a feel for them. If a seller has built up their Feedback selling antiques and collectables and then all of a sudden is selling a dozen plasma screens at a knock-down price, it is quite probable their account has been taken over.

Account hijacking is relatively rare and eBay has systems in place to protect buyers, but you should be alert too. If you think you have discovered a hijacked account, inform eBay's Customer Support.

Get in contact with the seller

If you want to be sure a seller is not dodgy, it is a good idea to get in touch with them. If you use the 'Ask Seller a Question' facility eBay will forward a message to them and they will be able to reply directly. Good sellers usually take the time to respond and answer questions. If you don't hear back from the seller this doesn't prove they are dodgy, but if they can't be bothered to reply to potential buyers via email then you are probably better off trading with another seller. A dubious reply can also be a good clue if the seller is dodgy.

Don't Trade 'off eBay'

Some unsuspecting people get ripped off because they see an item on eBay and get in touch with the seller, who then offers to sell them the item in a private transaction, 'off eBay'. If you don't buy your item on eBay you are not protected by the site's protection programmes and cannot leave or receive Feedback for the transaction. If you are the victim of a fraud in such an instance, you will have no recourse to eBay.

Go with Your Instincts

As in the offline world, your best tool for trading safely is your common sense. If there is something not quite right about the listing, the seller or the item and you don't feel comfortable, don't bid. The beauty of eBay is that there are always other sellers and other items. Obviously there are bargains to be had, but the old maxim still stands: 'If it's too good to be true then it probably is.'

Paying Safely

Paying safely on eBay is the key to having a successful trade. The safest way to pay is by using PayPal because of the Buyer Protection Programme it has in place. Essentially, PayPal will guarantee your money when you buy from reputable sellers. However, not all sellers use PayPal and you should be aware of the potential dangers represented by other payment methods.

You want your payment to be secure and trackable so that you can follow up if a seller disputes receiving it or get your money back if the item never arrives.

Cash is a very insecure way of paying if you are sending it in the post. It is not insured and you will have no recourse if it is lost. Indeed, you have no confirmation it has arrived safely except the recipient's word.

Avoid sellers who will only accept Western Union payments: it's a hallmark of a dodgy seller. It is difficult to track such payments and eBay advises that you don't use Western Union for payments either within the UK or abroad.

Cheques are reasonably safe to send as payment within the UK because they are trackable and banks are required to keep records. In the unlikely event of a problem you will be able to follow up with the banks and you can also cancel a cheque if the need arises.

Escrow

If any item is very expensive or the price you are willing to pay is dependent on the condition of the item, you may not be willing to take a leap into the unknown. At times like this you might want to use an escrow service.

An escrow service is a middleman who ensures that you, as a buyer, are protected. Here's how it works. You agree with the seller that you will use an escrow service to complete the transaction. You send payment to the escrow company, which informs the seller that the money has been received. The seller then despatches the item you have bought directly to you. Once you have received the item, you confirm that the item is as you expected and the escrow service releases the money to the seller.

eBay recommends escrow.com as a reputable service. The basic cost of its service, which is usually met by the buyer, is £15. You should avoid other escrow services because they can sometimes be used by fraudsters. Even if a site has the eBay logo it could be dodgy: eBay only recommends escrow.com.

Account Safety

As an eBay buyer and seller you need to take precautions to protect your eBay and PayPal accounts. As already discussed, there is a risk that someone will try to take over your accounts and use them for fraudulent activity.

Spoofs and Scams

You will have heard on the news about fake emails being sent out by fraudsters targeting online banking customers. By tricking people into giving out personal details, they hope to take control of people's bank accounts for fraudulent purposes. Spoof emails and fake websites are also used in attempts to take over established eBay members' accounts for other people's fraudulent activities.

An eBay account with good Feedback is a valuable commodity that other people prize. If you have taken the time and effort to build up your reputation, you won't want to jeopardise it. Although the risk of such a takeover is small, being aware of the activity diminishes the chance of it happening to you.

• **Identifying spoofs** Spoof emails can look deceptively like official eBay emails. However, they are in fact pretty easy to distinguish from the genuine articles. The purpose of these emails is to trick you into revealing your personal details so that the fraudsters can use your account to set up fake listings on eBay and rip off unsuspecting buyers. These emails will typically ask you to sign in to your eBay account in the main body of the mail. eBay will never ask you to sign in via an email; it will always direct you to the eBay site. Also eBay will never ask you to provide credit card details, PIN or any other personal details in emails like this. These emails will sometimes include threatening messages saying that your eBay account is about to be suspended and eBay needs you to confirm your details. eBay never asks you to confirm your details in such a way.

• **Fake websites** Sometimes a spoof email will direct you to a fake website and ask you to sign in there. Fake websites try to look like eBay so that you will be tricked into giving your details. There are clues that betray them, for example the URL at the top of the page will not be a genuine eBay URL.

• **The eBay Toolbar** One way to be certain you are signing into a genuine eBay page is to install the eBay Toolbar. This sits at the top of your internet browser and means you can easily access the eBay site wherever you are on the net. It also has some very useful safety features.

If you are on a genuine eBay or PayPal site, an icon in the Toolbar will show green and you're safe to sign in. If you are on a site that might look like eBay but isn't, then the Toolbar will show as grey if the site is unknown or red if it is a known spoof site. If the Toolbar shows as red or grey you shouldn't sign in because your personal information will be at risk.

As an additional safety feature, if you attempt to sign in to a site the Toolbar doesn't recognise as eBay using your eBay password, the toolbar will inform you. To get the Toolbar go to http://www.ebay.co.uk/ebay_toolbar.

- **What if I receive a spoof email?** If you have received a spoof and recognised it, you are perfectly safe as long as you haven't filled in any details. eBay works with law enforcement agencies all over the world to track down and prosecute the senders of spoof emails. The emails themselves contain vital information that eBay can use to trace their origin. Therefore if you receive a spoof email you should send it to eBay. Simply forward the email to spoof@ebay.co.uk and eBay will do the rest. If you receive a PayPal spoof send it to spoof@paypal.com.

- **What do I do if I fall for a spoof?** If you do submit your details to a fake site after receiving a spoof email, you will have to act quickly. First, you should change your password so that the information you have accidentally provided is no longer valid. If you have submitted credit card details or bank information, then you should contact the credit card issuer or your bank immediately.

eBay is constantly updating its information about spoof emails and fake websites. You can find the full and up-to-date details here:

http://pages.ebay.co.uk/education/spooftutorial/index.html

The eBay Discussion Boards are also an invaluable source of information about the latest scam emails doing the rounds. If you have received a spoof the chances are that hundreds of other people will have received one too. You can consult with other members on the boards and also warn others who have received a spoof email but might not have identified it.

Password Security

As long as your password is safe, your eBay account is secure and only for your personal use. Considering this, it is amazing how lax some people are when it comes to protecting their password. There are a few easy ways to keep your password safe and your eBay account secure.

Create a 'Good' Password

In addition to scam or spoof emails, your account is also at risk from hacking using advanced computer programs. These keep trying to log in to your account using possible passwords until they find the right one. eBay has security systems in place to try to thwart this sort of activity, but if you have another internet account with the same password then your eBay account is at risk.

One thing you can do is to use a password that is very difficult to guess. Never use a word that is in a dictionary or obviously related to your User ID. Also avoid things related to your life such as a birth date, pet's name or hobby. Use a combination of upper- and lower-case letters and numbers to create a password that is almost uncrackable. Six characters will do, but eight or ten are better.

For instance, 'password' is a very insecure password. But if you change it so it is 'Pa55w0rD' or 'p@sSW0r6' it is significantly more secure. Be creative and your password will be safer from the hackers.

Another idea is to use total gibberish. Take a phrase or lyric you find easy to recall, such as 'There's an old mill by the stream, Nellie Dean'. Take the first letter of each word and you have 'taombtsnd'. Some of these letters can be capitalised. Some can be exchanged for numbers and others for punctuation marks or other characters and you could end up with 'T@om8+Snd'. Obviously, don't use this example but make up your own.

- **Keep your password secret** Never write your password down or give it to anyone else. The safest place for your password is in your head.

- **Change it on a regular basis** There is no need to change it daily or even weekly, but by changing your password on a

regular basis you are moving the goalposts for those who
want to get their hands on your account.

• **Use different passwords for eBay and PayPal** If your
eBay account or PayPal account is hacked then the chances
are that the hackers will try to use the password for one
account on the other. After all, there's a good chance they
will be the same. It is advisable to use different passwords
for PayPal and eBay and for other online accounts. It may
seem like a chore, but it will be much more irritating to have
to regain control of your accounts if they are taken over.

The Safety Centre

eBay provides up-to-date safety information. It's worth taking the
time to inform yourself and learn how to minimise the risks when
you are trading on the site.

The Safety Centre can be accessed via a link at the base of
the Home Page and at this address:

http://pages.ebay.co.uk/safetycentre/index.html

Inside Information:
eBay Addiction

*Beware of eBay addiction. You might be laughing at the very
idea as you read this, but everyone is vulnerable. Research
papers have been written on the subject; psychologists in
America recognise it as a genuine condition. Otherwise
normal and balanced people can succumb to eBay addiction
in the same way people become addicted to cybersex or
gambling. Seriously.*

*The following behaviour might suggest you are addicted to
eBay:*

*• **Bidding over the odds for an item you don't really want
or need** This happens a lot. You see an item you quite like
but don't really want or need. You put in a little bid and fully
expect to get outbid, and of course someone else comes
along and outbids you. But you don't like being outbid so*

you place another bid, trying to outbid the other bidder. You outbid them and then they outbid you again. You bid again and again and they outbid you again and again until it becomes a war. You have to beat the other bidder at all costs and it doesn't matter that you are paying over the odds for some bit of over-priced tat: you have to be the winner. And when the auction ends you feel a surge of satisfaction, triumph and pride. Until you have to pay, when you realise quite how much of your hard-earned cash you have shelled out and you know the item wasn't worth it. Then when it arrives you have to lie about how much it cost in case your loved ones think you have totally lost the plot. Both self-reproach and dishonesty are classic signs of an addict.

• **Getting up in the middle of the night to place a last-minute bid** *Many eBay buyers like to watch an item and wait until the last minute before they bid. Bidding early just pushes the price up, they think. Of course, you can get computer programs that will bid for you while you sleep. But the eBay addict doesn't get their fix from a program, so they get up in the middle of the night to place their bid and enjoy the exhilaration of winning. The next day is spent in an exhausted daze.*

• **Buying items just because they're worth more if you sell them on eBay** *A trip to a car boot sale or charity shop can be heaven for an eBay addict. As they peruse the stalls and shelves they seek out items they think they can sell for more on eBay. Even if they only gain an extra quid or two, the satisfaction and victory are tangible. The money isn't the issue, it is the knowledge that they have outwitted the original seller. With a smug feeling of superiority they will snap up some trinket or bauble, murmuring to themselves with a strange maniacal look in their eyes, 'I'll get more for this on eBay.'*

• **Free Listing Days madness** *Every now and again eBay holds a Free Listing Day. You don't get much notice, but for one day only eBay doesn't charge Listing Fees. From the moment the Free Listing Day is announced until the clock strikes midnight and it is over, the addict goes into overdrive. Children are left unfed, dogs go unwalked and partners sit neglected as the addict scurries round the house* *trying to find things to list to take advantage of the event. Anything that is not nailed down is at risk from the eBay addict gripped by Free Listing Day fever. Photographs are taken, descriptions written and the addict will often stay up late making sure they take full advantage. They are satisfied but others look on bemused: was the total saving of £7 on Listing Fees really worth it?*

• *Your house is full of rubbish* *You can't throw out anything without wondering whether a) you could sell it on eBay or b) use it as packaging when you send out eBay sales.*

• *Thinking murderous thoughts when you get negative Feedback* *Surf the pain. Get over it. It doesn't last long. Telling the judge that you killed someone because they left you negative Feedback won't protect you.*

19
Finding Help, Friendship and Love on eBay

One guy was really glad he was able to find help from other community members on eBay. He used eBay from his garden shed and late one night he managed to get himself locked in. Unable to attract the attention of neighbours, he posted a message on the eBay Community Boards including the phone number of his local police station and his address, hoping someone would call the coppers so they could come round and release him. When the police arrived they told him they had been alerted by a call from an eBay member in America.

Odd as it may sound, some people also find friendship and love on eBay. One lady I heard about sold a comic on eBay and was surprised to discover it had been bought by a woman who lived just down the road. Needless to say, the seller popped a few doors down to deliver it and they were delighted to discover a shared interest in Japanese Manga. Despite their proximity they had never spoken but soon they struck up a firm friendship.

At eBay Live! (eBay's annual Community Conference in the USA) in 2004 a couple who had met on eBay were married and there are some examples of people who have found love closer to home. One regular on the UK chatboards actually moved to the United States to live with a man she met on the site and they are now married. Another pair have recently moved in with each other after meeting on the Discussion Boards. I spoke to one woman who met her boyfriend after she sold him a rare punk record. They lived in the same town and both thought they were the only punk fans in the area until their transaction; they plan to get married. And they say romance is dead.

Glossary

About Me page A page created by an eBay member that tells the community more about them.

Announcement Board Where eBay informs the community about changes to the site,

Auction Buy It Now An auction with a Buy It Now option too. The Buy It Now option disappears when the first bid is placed.

Auction format The traditional eBay selling format, where members bid against each other and the highest bidder wins the item.

AuctionWeb The original name of eBay.

Bid increments The steps by which bids increase.

Browsing Finding items to buy by looking through categories.

Buy It Now A way of buying and selling that doesn't require bidding but where an item can be purchased instantly at a fixed price determined by the seller.

Checkout The largely automated process a buyer passes through at the end of a listing that enables them to pay the seller and pass their contact details to them.

Community The collective term for all the members of eBay.

Community Boards Chat boards provided by eBay so the community can interact with one another and eBay staff.

Deadbeat bidder Someone who bids but doesn't pay.

Dutch auction A multiple-item auction format that means that the multiple bidders pay the lowest possible price.

EPS eBay Picture Services

Feedback Reviews left by eBay members about and for other members.

Final Value Fee The commission that sellers pay to eBay for a successful sale, based on a percentage of the final price.

Fixed price Another name for Buy It Now, where there is no bidding and buyers pay a price fixed by the seller.

Gallery A listing enhancement that allows buyers to catch a glimpse of an item on a Listings Page before clicking on the Item Title.

Insertion Fees Another name for Listing Fees: the fees for placing an item for sale on eBay.

Item Description The written description a seller gives an item.

Item Specifics Information about an item (such as size, brand or condition) that a seller can choose when listing an item that allows buyers to locate it using the Product Finder.

Item Title The one-line description a seller gives an item to attract buyers.

Listing An advert on eBay.

Listing Designer Template A service offered by eBay on the Sell Your Item form that allows sellers to make their listings more attractive.

Listing Enhancement A paid-for option to make your listing more prominent in Listings Pages.

Listing Fees The fees for placing an item for sale on eBay.

Listings Pages Pages where the items that match your Search or Browse requirements are displayed.

Member Profile A detailed digest of a member's Feedback and history on eBay. Accessed by clicking on the member's Feedback score (the number next to their User ID).

My eBay A personalised list of your eBay buying and selling activities that is automatically updated. You can also use My eBay to access your Account details and leave Feedback.

NARU Not A Registered User: eBay slang for someone who has been suspended from the site.

Navigation Bar The links at the top of a page that you use to get to other parts of the eBay site.

Negative Feedback An unfavourable review of another eBay member after a trade.

Neutral Feedback A neither favourable nor unfavourable review of another member, but considered by many eBay members to be nearly as bad as negative Feedback.

PayPal An online payment system integrated with the eBay site.

Pierre Omidyar eBay's founder.

Positive Feedback A favourable review of an eBay member.

PowerSeller A seller recognised by eBay for selling a significant amount of stuff and maintaining high standards of conduct.

Privacy Policy eBay's promises to you that govern how it manages the personal details that you submit when you register.

Product Finder The tool a buyer uses on Listings Pages to sort item by values assigned to them by sellers, such as brand, size and condition.

Proxy Bidding The automatic bidding system that means eBay will bid on your behalf up to your maximum, depending on the other bids placed.

Reserve Price A price that can be added to a listing by the seller that means they can have a low Starting Price to encourage bidding but don't have to sell unless the Reserve Price is met. The Reserve Price is not revealed to bidders.

Scheduled Listings The option to create a listing but request that eBay delays sending it to the site until a time of your choosing.

Searching Finding items on eBay by putting keywords into the Search engine.

Sell Your Item form The online form where you enter information about your item so eBay can build your listing.

Seller Information Box A section on the View Item page that summarises a selling member's details.

Selling Manager An advanced version of My eBay that is useful if you are selling numerous items. It's free.

Selling Manager Pro More advanced than Selling Manager, this is a listing and management tool for high-volume sellers.

Shill bidding When a seller bids up their own item to inflate the price. Shill bidding is prohibited on eBay.

Site Map Accessed from the Navigation Bar, the Site Map is an index of the pages on eBay.

Sniping Bidding in the final seconds of a listing.

Spoof emails Emails that appear to come from eBay and aim to trick you into revealing your personal information.

Starting Price The price you start the bidding at on a listing.

Subtitle A listing enhancement that allows you to add more detail to an Item Title.

Turbo Lister An offline program that eBay provides to help you create listings in bulk and upload them to eBay in one go without using the Sell Your Item form.

User Agreement The contract between a member and eBay that you agree to when you join eBay.

User ID The unique name that you are identified by on eBay.

URL A web address such as http://www.ebay.co.uk.

View Item page An eBay listing or advert.

Watch List A buyer can add an item to their Watch List and the item will be stored in My eBay so they can bid at a later date if they want.

Thanks

At eBay.co.uk many members of staff have been generous with their time, expertise, suggestions and encouragement. In particular I am grateful to Amy, Tanya, Tony G., Nicky A., Jo G., Paul D., Jon, Paul W, Elspeth, Garreth, Victoria, David W., Ian J., Matt P., Doug Mc., Rob M., Bev, Henry and Alexia to name but a few.

Thanks are also due to my parents, Clive and Muriel, who are always supportive and encouraging. Neil Ford has put up with too much grumpiness but never once complained when asked to proofread and critique. Dave O'Callaghan too has been an unstinting source of support. Sarah Prag, Ruth Elkins, Vanessa Gordon-Dseagu and Kate Saunders all offered much encouragement, feedback and moral support. My agent Robert Dudley and Nick, Stephen, Victoria and Sally at Nicholas Brealey Publishing have been patient and understanding towards this first-time author. Jennifer Mowat, eBay.co.uk's first Managing Director, also asked to be mentioned, and I am delighted to do so. All the advice on safe passwords is dedicated to Danielle Radojcin.

I am also grateful to the thousands of eBay members I have met and spoken to over the years. Many have offered their time, comments and experiences freely and helped me understand what a new member on eBay needs. Particular thanks are due to the members who frequent the eBay Discussion Boards and never let me ignore their views and thoughts: the eBay community is a daily delight and inspiration.

Dan Wilson